SHOWERED BY GRACE

IRIS LONG

Hunter Heart Publishing
Colorado Springs, Colorado

SHOWERED BY GRACE

IRIS LONG

Name, with gratitude,

Grace

His under

Luke 1:37

Showered By Grace

To order products, or for any other correspondence:

Hunter Heart Publishing
4164 Austin Bluffs Parkway, Suite 214
Colorado Springs, Colorado 80918
www.hunterheartpublishing.com
Tel. (253) 906-2160 – Fax: (719) 368-6655
E-mail: publisher@hunterheartpublishing.com
Or reach us on the internet: www.hunterheartpublishing.com
"Offering God's Heart to a D ying World"

This book and all other Hunter Heart Publishing™ Eagle's Wings
Press™ and Hunter Heart Kids™ books are available at Christian
bookstores and distributors worldwide.

Chief Editor: Gord Dormer
Book cover design: Phil Coles Independent Design
Front cover photo by: Jim Morris Photography, Tuscaloosa, AL
Layout & logos: Exousia Marketing Group www.exousiamg.com
ISBN: 978-1722722050
Printed in the United States of America.

DEDICATION

GOD
for Your abounding love, mercy, and grace

Michael and Miranda
beloved treasures in my heart

Scott
for your complete and perfect love and devotion

"As he went along, he saw a man blind from birth. His disciples asked
him, "Rabbi, who sinned, this man or his parents, that he was born
blind?"
"Neither this man nor his parents sinned," said Jesus, "but this happened so that the works of God might be displayed in him."
John 9:1-3 NIV

ACKNOWLEDGMENTS

There are no coincidences in the life of a believer, and each person on this page has played a vital role in my journey. I cannot thank you enough and I pray God will bless you abundantly. God bless anyone I have not mentioned specifically whose path crossed mine. These are listed in random order.

Hunter Heart Publishing Company, for offering the book publishing contest, providing the opportunity to share my story with the world. Thank you for your guidance and support in all aspects of this book.

Sue H, for your loving heart. You went above and beyond, and I was blessed incredibly through your unselfish sacrifice, helping me multiple times through stressful circumstances. Thank you for your prayers and your love. Our time at "The Electric Brew" was a special gift from God. Thank you to your small group friends as well for the extra hands.

Chris E and the Team Construction Family, for your overwhelming generosity of hand and heart. God bless you, Chris, for your role as a mentor, friend, and employer to Scott. Thank you does not cover the sacrifice of your time and efforts on my behalf after he moved to heaven.

Pastor Jeremiah Olson, for your prayers, kindness, and generosity of heart. Thank you for your comforting words at Scott's funeral and for your warm greetings at church. You hold a special place in my heart.

Grace Community Church, for godly teaching. God continued to minister to me through GCC after Scott moved to heaven. Thank you to Pastor Jim Brown for a beautiful wedding ceremony and to his wife, Anne, for being a part of one of the happiest days of my life. I appreciate your continued prayers.

Ellis Shetler and Yoder-Culp Funeral Home in Goshen, for your helpful assistance, kindness, and guidance through the arrangements and service. Thank you for your thoughtfulness and generosity to plant a tree in Scott's memory. The grief counseling you provided was a blessing and helped me tremendously.

Special friends: Rachel H, Peggy L, Maureen B, Nicole B, Nadine M, Shirley and Robert C, Joyce Y, Arlene and David K, Sharon S, Jean K, Kay and Lil M, for your outpouring of love and support, for your generosity, and for your prayers and friendship.

Neighbors in Goshen: Levi and Ruth B, Red and Amanda N, Jim and Sandy B, Don and Denette S, The Fiqueroas, Ron and Jackie P, Deb O, for your friendship, your concern, your kindness, and your prayers. Thank you for bringing food and checking on me, for sharing a cup of coffee, for help with the lawn, for caring.

My grief family, Petunia's Pals: Beverley L, George T, Patricia N, Fred S, Susie S, for your friendship, love, and prayers. Our time of fellowship together was special and healing, and those memories are a treasure in my heart.

Sid and Cindy Slabaugh of Goshen, for your kindness and faithfulness to return Scott's class ring. God placed it in the hands of trustworthy servants. Thank you.

Rosalie D, for the prayers, support, and the timely spiritual guidance I needed immediately following Scott's move to heaven. Thank you for your concern.

Margaret C, for your kindness, conversation, and prayers. Thank you for reaching out to me and sharing meals and memories.

Mary G, for your friendship and compassionate heart. God spoke to me through the devotional book and booklet that you sent, confirming the timing of my move to Tennessee. The member directory from my childhood neighborhood church was a beautiful blessing that touched me deeply.

Teri E and Rita B, for sharing my tears and pain during the worst years. Thank you for your loving hearts and compassion and for all your help in my life at that time.

Anita L, for your continued steadfast friendship, for your countless prayers on my behalf, for your loyalty in the workplace, for attending our wedding and visiting after Scott died, for all the shared memories.

Christina E, for your unwavering faithfulness and love. Your encouragement and prayers for my family and me have lifted and carried me through the past two years. God sent a beautiful faithful servant with a warrior heart for spiritual guidance and support, and I am truly thankful.

Mrs. Gregory and Ms. Newman, for demonstrating the heart of Jesus to a lost, unhappy, awkward child. Thank you for your loving kindness.

The women of the Plan B small group at FPC, for your support, prayers and encouragement. Thank you for your friendship and love in helping me adjust after my move to Knoxville and through my grief at that time.

Jim Morris Photography, "Oak Arches," for the profound impact your photo has had on my life. I enjoyed our conversations on the phone and appreciate the history behind the photo.

TABLE OF CONTENTS

PROLOGUE

The idea to write this book came from God, first planted as a soft seed, while still grieving in Goshen in 2011. During a conversation with Sue at the coffee house, I made the statement, "God has given me a beautiful love story to tell!" I felt a stirring in my spirit as I spoke those words, but they were overshadowed by my grief and events of daily life at that time. My grief journey continued, and I started praying for God to reveal His plan for my life. About three months after I moved to Knoxville, I was watching a Christian message on T.V. one evening by Jentezen Franklin who was speaking about assignment, purpose, and destiny. The message spoke to me personally, and I tucked handwritten notes into my Bible. In February of 2013, God told me to write this book, and I was reminded of my words spoken in Goshen in the Fall of 2011. When I protested that I did not know how to write a book and that I did not know what the book should contain, He said, "Tell people what I have done for you. Tell the story simply, without interpretation or preaching."

The prospect of digging up old memories from my childhood and the past, as well as revisiting my grief after Scott's move to heaven, was overwhelming, and I was filled with a sense of dread. I liked the idea of just sharing my love story with Scott, but God reminded me that this story was more than just a romantic relationship between a man and a woman. God's amazing love and abundant grace were far more powerful and needed to be shared with others as well. I would have to delve into all the pain of the past and bring the details out into the open. If I tried to cover the dirt and just skim over the specifics, the effectiveness of the book would be diminished. This was an assignment from God that required obedience.

My initial excitement quickly fizzled, as I struggled to make any progress with the writing. My job was demanding with a heavy work-load, and I was left with little energy or enthusiasm for writing at the end of the day. Weekends were spent resting and preparing for the week ahead with housework and other chores. Occasionally, after spiritual prodding, I would write a page or two on notebook paper; whatever memory came to mind, without any order or plan. The prompting was so insistent at times that I had no rest until I wrote. Every evening I wres-tled with guilt if I did not write. This ongoing spiritual battle brought increased fatigue and stress over the next several months. Through a series of events, God showed me that every command from Him comes with a choice. He would not force me to choose obedience. I could obey and receive the promises He had spoken to me, or I could continue on in disobedience and suffer any consequences. I believed God's promises, and I wanted to obey Him, because I understood that there was great blessing attached, with increased spiritual growth, revelation, and deeper intimacy with God. This assignment would lead to another in the future. I wanted to receive every blessing He had planned for my life and for others who would be impacted, as well.

My job was slated to end initially in early 2014, as my position would no longer be required. I was preparing mentally for this change and planned to start writing full-time, until completion of the book once my employment was terminated. Though I trusted God to provide my needs, I battled the fear of the unknown. I had worked full-time since I was 17 years old and for many years in the past, employment had been my sole source of security. I had given my job responsibilities priority over everything else in life during those years, because of the need to support myself and cover my living expenses alone. God reminded me that when He had tried to work in my life in 1999, I ran back to what was familiar in fear with disastrous results, and I was in danger of repeating those same mistakes.

I reaffirmed my faith in God and looked forward to this change in my life. Within the last two weeks of employment, which had been extended until June, I was unexpectedly offered extra work and the opportunity to continue my job as an independent contractor. I was now standing at the fork in the road. Would I stay employed with a guaranteed paycheck and insurance coverage, or would I obey God and trust Him to provide all my needs? I had worked for the same physician for sixteen years, and I reflected back on my past attitude about my job and all the changes I had moved through during this employment. I also remembered God's faithfulness and love, my rescue from the pit and the darkness, the grace He had showered over me in spite of my behavior and decisions, and the amazing love I had shared with Scott. The next morning, I submitted my letter of resignation to the office administrator. There was a definite lift in my spirit, as I hit the "send" button on my keyboard. My last day of employment was July 4, 2014, Independence Day.

This book would not have progressed without the prayer warrior God sent into my life. I met Christina in late January of 2013 at Faith Promise Church. I had started attending this church in mid-November on the Sunday following my move to Knoxville. An Internet search of contemporary Christian churches in my area had led me to Faith Promise, and after attending for several weeks, I signed up for the Next Steps Class.

Christina was serving as a table host during this informational meeting regarding the church history, vision, and values. She was very warm and friendly, and I felt a spiritual connection with her that day, though it was unclear how we would interact in the future. In May, she phoned me to ask if I would be interested in participating in a life coaching project required for her Master's degree. Without hesitation, I agreed. I remembered that moment of connection in January and recognized that God was moving in this situation. Our next phone conversation began an incredible journey. Over the following months, our relationship expanded far beyond the class requirement. There were many parallels in our walk with God, and sometimes, those lines crisscrossed or ran perpendicular, but remained connected, and we both realized that God was working in us and through us for His purpose and our mutual good. She has been a faithful prayer warrior and powerful intercessor for my family and me. God has spoken to her countless times to lift me in prayer for specific needs. Likewise, He has ministered to her through my story and my experiences with Him. We have laughed and cried together, as we shared amazing revelations. She is a Godsend, a true treasure in my heart, a genuine friend. She has encouraged me and emailed reminder messages when prompted by God to keep me on track. God spoke reassurance through her for His provision, while writing this book.

Amazingly, after two weeks of writing full time, I had completed seventy-two typed pages, whereas during the previous six months, I had written only a small stack of pages in a notebook. Each day before writing, I prayed and asked the Holy Spirit to guide my thoughts and to give me His words. Sometimes, at night or early in the morning, He would bring to mind certain memories to include, or He would direct me to add details to an incident that I had not focused on originally. Writing this book has been a journey within a journey, with further spiritual catharsis of the pain, lies, and hopelessness of my past. This season of spiritual growth and the revelations from the Holy Spirit have brought pain, as well as healing. My joy and delight come from God, and I ask every day to see Him and to hear from Him, seeking wisdom and discernment daily. He has awakened in me the need and hunger for more of Him. There is no greater thrill than a surprise touch from above!

God led me to the Land of Goshen for love, healing, and the beginning of my journey. I have been rescued from destruction, from the bottom of the pit, and from the enemy through His amazing love and grace. God has given me life, salvation, purpose, peace, joy, and a beautiful love story to tell.

Come and journey with me,

Iris

Chapter One

THE DREAM

When I woke up that morning on my birthday in 2005, I knew my life was going to change; something wonderful was going to happen and everything was going to be different. I did not hear any voices or receive any cryptic messages; rather, it was as though my entire self--mind, body, and spirit--knew that life was never going to be the same. In amazement, I asked God, out loud, if this was from Him. Incredible joy and strength flooded through me in response, followed immediately by a rush of mounting doubt. Why would God bless me at this point in my life since I had rebelled, disobeyed, and left Him out of my life for the most part? I was saved and baptized when I was twelve years old, but had not grown in my faith or developed a relationship with God since that time.

My best friend and her family had recently helped me move into a very nice apartment. The large complex was situated outside the city in a quiet and peaceful area, only a few miles from shopping centers and grocery stores. The view from my spacious balcony was unobstructed and pleasant. There were many buildings in the complex and some were situated close together; however, a retention pond protected the wide open space in front of my balcony. In the distance, an occasional train whistle would blow. The highway was far enough away that traffic noise was minimal. This was the largest and nicest apartment I had lived in since my divorce, and I was very happy with this change of address. For the first time in many years, I was comfortable in my own place.

Life had settled down almost ten years later. The divorce and its aftermath had left me devastated financially, emotionally, and spiritually. I was better situated financially, and my children were young adults pursuing their own lives. I was ready to meet someone for a serious relationship, but I did not have many friends and my workplace offered no options. I had never been a bar or party person, so those were checked off the list of possibilities. A friend suggested that I start going to church to try to meet someone, but I was not comfortable with the idea of attending church for the wrong motives. I spent a lot of time on the computer both at work and at home, and Internet dating seemed like a good idea.

Desiring to meet a believer, I opted to join a Christian site, believing that predators of any kind would be too cheap to pay and would stick to the free sites. My membership proved very disappointing. The matches I received were all located several hundred miles away. Decreasing the distance parameters in the search yielded very few matches, and none of those resulted in a meeting. Disappointed with the lack of a match, I decided to try a non-Christian site that was free. There were several matches right away, and I was filled with the excitement and anticipation of a new beginning. I persisted in Internet dating for more than a year off and on, but each man I met was more disappointing than the previous. Some claimed to believe in God, but were not walking with Him. A sense of desperation was very strong in some of the men, underlining my own loneliness and isolation. Many of the matches consisted of only email messages and did not progress to an actual meeting. The men who said they were looking for a relationship were only looking for sex, for emotional or financial rescue, or for help battling their exes with child support and control issues. I had no energy and no desire to fight anyone else's battles, and I was not looking to take care of anyone. A few men were honest on the front end that they were only looking to fulfill specific sexual desires and were not interested in a relationship. Other men were more interested in my assets than my personality, and their messages centered on home ownership, job title, retirement/savings, and other monetary definers. I would typically present a much lower income profile than my actual status, which was effective in closing those conversations. I was not impressed by shallow men who defined themselves solely by their income and possessions or position. Regardless of the situation, I discovered that the men I met hid their true motives, until the first meeting, and they all proved to be disappointing.

The energy and time I expended on each new match was exhausting. These typically started with an email notice that I had received new matches, followed by email messages, possibly moving forward to instant messenger or a phone call, and then onto a meeting. These steps varied in length, and most of the communication ended before a phone call or a meeting. It was an emotional roller coaster, with anticipation building, while climbing that first hill and then coasting in the excitement of possibility, until the ride ended in disappointment or disaster.

I continued on this Internet dead-end, as though this was my only option to meet someone. Through the following months, with my growing disappointment and doubts that any decent man would be interested in me, I lowered my standards. Instead of believing for the best, I settled for whatever came my way. Prince Charming was not going to knock on my door with a glass slipper. The dream I experienced on my birthday in 2005 had faded as life continued the same through the following months. Occasionally, I would think about that day and wonder if I should stop the Internet dating, but there was a voice telling me that if God was going to bless me, He would keep His word and to continue as I was doing in the meantime. This reassurance appealed to me and allowed me to continue interacting through the dating site.

As I had become more comfortable with this process, I also became less cautious, and I lost sight of my initial desire to meet a godly man. I had been exchanging messages with one man in particular and we set up a date to meet at a local restaurant. Dinner and conversation were pleasant, though not especially interesting, and afterwards, he asked if I would like to go for a ride. With only slight hesitation, I agreed and got into his truck. Riding around mindlessly with this man for a while seemed more appealing than going home alone early. He drove out of town for several miles while we talked; however, at one point, I felt a slight sense of alarm and started praying. I suddenly realized how far away we were from the restaurant, and I was in unfamiliar territory on an unknown highway. He eventually turned around and brought me back to my car safely and unharmed, and I thanked God for His protection as I drove home. Later, as I was reflecting over the evening, I thought about all the things that could have happened to me in that vulnerable situation, and I was thankful, again, for my safety.

I hit rock bottom with the last man I met on the dating site. I did not know him very well, as we had only exchanged a few messages. We agreed to meet at a local restaurant and after an appetizer; I followed him back to his hotel and had sex with him. There was a moment that I could have escaped, but I did not seize that window of opportunity, and I followed this man, as though I had no choice. I was not particularly attracted to him, and I felt no connection to him on any level. I was weary from the hopelessness, loneliness, rejection, and the same negative thoughts of my past running through my mind. My life was empty, and it did not matter what I did. The only purpose for my existence was to work and pay bills.

Overwhelming shame consumed me as he walked me back to my car a little later. The parking lot was full of people and vehicles, with a lot of activity going on that I was only vaguely aware of as I quickly opened the door to my vehicle and locked the doors. I wanted to get as far away from him and this place as possible. I was in a state of mental panic as I drove home. All of the thoughts that had encouraged me to meet this man were now condemning me with guilt and shock. The realization of what I had just done kept slamming me. The level I had sunk to was crushing and I could hardly breathe. I showered as soon as I got home, but I was still dirty. Shame and disgust washed over me in waves and I wanted to hide. I could not face God. I was crying and angry at myself for my weakness when a moment of escape presented itself and I failed to take it. I could not blame my behavior on alcohol or drugs, as I had never used those, and I was left with nothing to blame but my same weak defeated self.

The condemnation from my own thoughts was pounding relentlessly in my head and I was filled with terror. My heart and mind were racing with fear and self-loathing. I had no value and I was of no consequence to anyone. Unable to sit or lie down, I paced and sobbed, afraid that I was going to die and go to hell. My soul was in mortal danger. I had never known such fear as I experienced throughout the rest of that night into the morning, as I removed the dating site profiles, pictures, email addresses, messages, and contacts.

I moved through the next few days expecting God to remove me from the earth in judgment. No man would ever love me, and I was going to spend the rest of my life alone. Looking for love and settling for lust, I had destroyed that dream of 2005. I buried myself in my work once again and shelved all hope of love and marriage.

Chapter Two

LOVE COMES KNOCKING

One night at home after signing out of my email account, I noticed a link on my homepage that piqued my curiosity. I clicked on the link, which led to a question and answer forum with countless categories covering a wide range of subjects. Intrigued, I clicked on the category for relationships/dating. I spent a couple of hours just reading questions and answers in that one section. After a few nights of only reading, I felt brave enough to answer a few questions and posted some questions of my own as well. I browsed through other categories and eventually landed in the entertainment section.

Every night after dinner, I would spend time in this forum, posting answers to interesting or fun questions. I followed some of the regular users and also noticed the users who frequently posted answers to my questions. In September of 2006, I became aware of a different partici-pant from the regulars, who was answering most of the questions I posted. I liked the way he expressed himself through his phrasing and words, as well as his values revealed through some of his answers. One day, I received a simple message from this user through the forum about something he had read in another question, and the next day, he mes-saged a reply to my response. I had the vague impression that there was something significant about this person. He had expressed the same beliefs that I held through his answers, and he was not crude or vulgar in his posts or messages. I spent a considerable amount of time reading through his past question and answer history. After a few days of messaging through the forum, he requested my email address so we could interact directly, if I felt comfortable. I agreed and we started messaging every day, both on the forum, as well as through email. We exchanged some personal information, and he asked that I email a photo. Skepticism rose when he said he did not have any recent pictures, as I had heard this same excuse while Internet dating and I told him I would not send a picture, until I received his photo. He borrowed a camera and set up a tripod to snap a picture of himself. The photo was less than optimal, as the lighting was not bright in the room, but at least now I could put a face to all the words we had shared. His name was Scott, he lived in Goshen, Indiana, and he was divorced. He was intelligent, quick witted, and a Christian.

My interest in Scott quickly accelerated. The highlight of my day was the time I spent in the forum with Scott and our emails. We moved to Instant Messenger, which added a more personal element to our communication. We had not spoken on the phone, and we did not have web cams--just our typed or handwritten words. As Thanksgiving was approaching, Scott had begun to talk about a face to face meeting. I was not afraid of him; however, I really enjoyed our communication and knew that if there was no chemistry when we met, we would not interact again on the forum or exchange any further messages. I was reluctant to risk our online friendship. He was willing to drive South 650 miles. Still, I hesitated. I did not want to feel guilty about his time and expense of traveling if our meeting was a disappointment, and I told him I was not ready to meet him in person. Undeterred, Scott then asked for my address, because he wanted to send me a "little friendship gift". I was not comfortable sharing my home address, and after some persuasion, I finally gave my work address. The package arrived a few days later on

December 5, 2006. Inside, I found a sweet friendship card and an adorable Lenox Christmas ornament, "A Glowing Friendship" of Rudolph and Hermey (the elf who wanted to be a dentist). Somewhere on the forum, he had read a post where I had mentioned that Rudolph the Red-Nosed Reindeer was one of my Christmas favorites. Warmth and reassurance about this man started to grow, as I read his handwritten words.

"Iris,

You beautifully personify your namesake; sharing messages from heaven to everyone you touch. In just the short time that I have known you, I have found in you a dear friend to cherish in my thoughts and in my heart!

God Bless You!
Scott"

I let Scott know when I received the card and gift, and I shared my delight for his thoughtfulness and generosity. He asked me to consider a meeting on his birthday, New Year's Day, and we continued to communicate via email and messages. The office where I worked held a Christmas open-house for employees and their spouses/families in mid-December. Scott had asked if I could email more pictures of me, and I explained that I did not have a camera, but would send a few pictures from this event, as the office administrator had posted multiple photos taken that evening on the company website to share with all the employees. A few days later, I received a package at work from Indiana. I opened it to find a beautiful gift box inside. An envelope rested on top of the box and enclosed I found the following letter, typed on Christmas letterhead.

"Dear Iris,

One of my elves has reported to me that an extremely important pho-to opportunity in your life was missed recently...something involving a black velvet dress. I wasn't able to understand all the details because my elf, Ernie, who witnessed this event, was left overwhelmed...stammering and trembling by what he has described as 'the purest form of beauty he has ever seen.' (It took us two days to calm him down!) Neverthe-less...we here at the North Pole find this tragedy of missed photo ops to be completely unacceptable for such a lovely young lady...and therefore, have taken immediate action to remedy the situation!

Enclosed is a gift for you...my hope is that another event in your life will not pass without record...so that those precious little moments can be forever remembered and cherished...by you, your family, and your friends. A smile like yours, dearest Iris, is a terrible thing to waste!

God bless you... and have a very Merry Christmas!!!

Sincerely,
Santa Claus"

Inside the box was a new Canon PowerShot digital camera. Aston-ished surprise was followed by vague uneasiness. I was very touched by the letter. This was the first and only letter from Santa I had ever re-ceived, and the words were clever and flattering. A part of me started to retreat in guilt that I did not deserve this present; however, a rush of reassurance filled me in response, pushing away all doubt and fear, and I accepted the words and the gift with glee and appreciation. I felt com-pelled to respond with a friendship Christmas card, as this gift deserved more than a thank-you via email. I spent a considerable amount of time in my search for the perfect card, sifting through countless cards to find the one that expressed genuine friendship and gratitude. There was a small picture of two cups of coffee on the front of the card. I added my own message inside the card.

"Scott,

In a short time, you have become a bright spot in my day. You are easy to talk to, to laugh and joke with, and a lot of fun to flirt with! I'm looking forward to discovering what else I like about you. I hope you and your family enjoy the holidays. You will be in my thoughts.

Iris"

By this time, I was more than a little curious about Scott. I wanted to talk to him, to hear his voice, and to spend some time in his company. I admired his faith and values, his sense of humor, and his balance of confidence and humility. The photo he had sent was not very flattering, as he was standing in a room without good lighting and his face was somewhat shadowed. It was taken at a distance for a full body shot and I could not see his face up close; however, my heart was touched by the friendship card and Santa letter, and my interest in him had increased. As the end of December approached, Scott persuaded me to meet him in person. The following days were filled with conflicting thoughts. Anticipation grew about meeting the man who had intrigued me with his words in the forum and in our messages, with his handwriting, and with his gifts. I wanted to know if the man in person matched the man I had met in my heart.

We discussed hotels in the area, and I gave him recommendations, as well as the local travel route and exits. We still had not spoken on the phone at this point. All of our communication was via email or Instant Messenger. He planned to leave early the next morning, to arrive around 7 p.m. I spent the day cleaning my apartment and preparing a meal for us to share upon his arrival. I received a call from Indiana at 6:30. As I answered the phone, I wondered if he was still at home. A woman's voice spoke in greeting and explained that she was Scott's mother; she was calling to let me know he had taken the wrong exit and would be about an hour late. Unfortunately, I had forgotten there were two exits off the interstate, and I had given the wrong exit in my instructions. He did not want to call me directly, as we were waiting until we met in person before we spoke, and had called his mother to phone me about the delay. The short conversation with her reassured me about meeting Scott, although the butterflies kept fluttering. I was a nervous wreck as the minutes of that final hour slowly crept by, checking my appearance in the mirror, straightening things in the apartment that I had already straightened countless times, and pacing through the rooms. All of a sudden, there was a knock. The moment had arrived. I opened the door and there stood this guy with a wonderful smile and beautiful blue eyes. I noted his appearance in a sweeping second--blue jeans, blue sweatshirt, and white tennis shoes, carrying a jacket--but my gaze was fixed on his face. He looked so much better than the photo he had emailed. WOW!!! I felt like a young girl on her first date. After inviting him in, we just stood in the living room looking at one another, trying to connect all we knew of each other with the person facing us. We spoke to one another for the first time. We sat down, still smiling in wonder, and started talking. We laughed and smiled and talked and talked and talked. I was lost in that smile, and awareness blossomed that something amazing was happening.

I had prepared a roast dinner in the slow cooker, and we stopped talking long enough to eat. While I was clearing away the dishes, Scott asked if I had any coffee. He looked at the canister I removed from the cabinet and then asked if he could brew some coffee he had brought with him. He came back into the kitchen carrying a bag of his favorite blend and a grinder. This was my first experience with fresh ground coffee, as I usually just bought a regular store brand, and I enjoyed watching him prepare and brew a pot. Time sped by as we continued talking and laughing after dinner, until suddenly, I realized that Scott had been driving more than eleven hours and was probably tired. I offered to let him stay at my place, as the hotel was more than ten miles away, and it was now late in the evening. He apparently had anticipated this possibility, because he had brought an air mattress, pillow and sheets! We laughed and somehow it seemed perfectly normal. It felt like I had known him all my life, though we had just met.

We spent the entire weekend talking, laughing, and smiling at each other. We visited a local Mississippi River museum, and I took him to the antique mall where I had maintained a booth as a vendor for the past four years. He was interested in everything about me, and I was not accustomed to so much undivided attention. I loved hearing his voice and listening to him speak. He seemed to enjoy my Southern accent, as I saw his lips twitch more than once while I was talking; however, to his credit, he did not mimic me or ask me to pronounce any words or phrases. Our conversation drifted in and around the questions and answers we had posted on the forum, our beliefs, our pasts, and our families. Time seemed to stand still for the entire visit. The rest of the world just faded and there was only Scott and me. Before he left, I knew that I was more than just fond of him, and I was in awe of this sudden change in my life.

He returned for a shorter visit two weeks later. On Saturday afternoon, we were discussing dinner plans as we sat on the loveseat. Scott rose and perched on the armrest. Taking my hand in his, he expressed his feelings for me. I shared my feelings for him in return, and we made a verbal commitment to one another. We reassured each other that we were only interested in our relationship and agreed not to engage in private messages on the forum or other Internet communication with members of the opposite sex. The same feelings I had experienced upon awakening from that dream in 2005 now flooded through my entire being, as I acknowledged that I was in love with Scott. We planned to see each other once a month from this point.

I did not share my relationship with Scott with my coworkers at first, only telling my daughter and son, because this love was too special for idle speculation. Whenever any questions or doubts rose in my mind, reassurance would quickly follow that I could trust this man and that his love was genuine.

In the years following my divorce, I had celebrated Valentine's Day by giving my children a basket filled with a card, candy, and small gifts. Valentine's Day 2007 was extra special. I was working at my desk when one of the secretaries, accompanied by a few other women in the office, approached me with a gorgeous arrangement of eighteen red roses and a mix of other flowers in a red crystal vase. My relationship with Scott was not yet common knowledge in the office, and they were full of questions. I offered a few details in response, while gazing at the beautiful flowers in delighted wonder. The card read, "Thinking of you always, my Valentine. Love, Scott." Happiness and love flooded over me, and I smiled brightly at those women waiting for more information.

Scott drove down a few days later for the weekend. He gave me a loving Valentine's card with its own special printed message; however, the best part was Scott's handwritten words covering the entire inside panel of the card. He took my breath away, as I read this message from his heart:

"Iris,

From the moment we first met in your doorway, my feelings for you have continued to grow deeper with each passing day. You have touched my life in ways I had never imagined possible with your beautiful soul, your warmth and kindness, your wonderful sense of humor, and your delightful conversation. The attraction and desire I have for you as a woman is sometimes overwhelming and oftentimes very exciting! To touch you, to feel your touch, and the intimacy we share is a magical experience like no other. You are truly an amazing woman...I feel blessed to have found you...I'm thankful that you opened your door and invited me into your life...and I'm looking forward to discovering everything about you and sharing many more wonderful moments with you!

Yours truly,
Scott"

Scott told me that he loved me with all his heart and asked if I would move to Goshen and become his wife. I told him I had fallen completely in love with him and that I would live anywhere with him as his wife. We discussed a timeline for this life change and agreed that I would move to Goshen in January of 2008. I left the moving details to Scott. I knew I could trust him and did not need to check behind him or prod him to take care of any arrangements. The focus of our time together was each other. We did not waste our conversation on the past or the future. We lived in the moment with joy and gratitude.

Through the following months, Scott continued to amaze and delight me with each new discovery of this man who in a very short time had captured my heart completely. We spoke on the phone every day after work and several times a day/night on the weekends. Everything he shared of himself, I treasured in my heart.

Scott and I continued to interact on the question and answer forum, occasionally posting answers to each other's questions. One day in April of 2007, a user posted a question, asking men how they know when they are in love and what finally happens to let them know they are in love. She wanted serious answers only. Scott did not typically answer this type of question, but he answered this one. I was overwhelmed reading the raw honesty of his words and amazed that he posted this in a public forum for all to see:

"WOW!!! I think the whole country just experienced a power surge from so many men shutting down their computers at the same time!!! I can tell you some of what I feel…but the rest I believe is a feeling that is truly indescribable and really never understood… at least not by me! I've always been leery of the idea of a 'Soul Mate', but if there is such a thing, I've found her!....the feelings associated with that is the part I don't understand, nor do I think I need to…I believe it comes from God and I don't question it. My feelings for her run so deep, it amazes me, thrills me, and scares me all at the same time! My mind and my body want to be close to her ALL the time!!! I feel completely comfortable with her in all situations and spending time with her is easy and fun. I love who she is and I respect her as a woman…intellectually, emotionally and sexually. I could go on and on about her endless good qualities….but I think the one thing for me that indicates true lasting love is the desire to care for her…to want good things for her and be willing to sacrifice for her. To be willing to accept the bad with the good, the better or the worse…love is a selfless act…the more selfless I feel, the deeper I feel my love for her. Her happiness touches me in places that have never before been touched!

In regards to what FINALLY happened to let me know this…I think I knew when she opened her door and I saw her face for the first time.

By the way…this person I love so much is Rainbow." (my nickname from Scott)

I read his words many, many times that day and in the following weeks and months, experiencing the same thrill from his words. I had never met a man like Scott. I loved him with all my heart, and I respected him and his core values. He sparked desire in me that I had never felt for anyone else, and I truly liked everything about this man. We connected in every way, and I was comfortable with him at all times.

Scott was eager for me to visit him in Indiana and to see his part of the world, before my eventual move in January, so we planned for my first visit for the third weekend in May of 2007. He mapped out my route and gave me specific instructions about the toll roads and the exits, and where to pay close attention to the signs. He had previously bought two pay-as-you-go mobile phones for us to use while traveling, since I would be driving alone. After checking my vehicle, he insisted on buying a new set of tires before my trip. I was moved tremendously by his thoughtfulness and concern for my safety. There had been no one to check on me or my vehicle in a long, long time. I felt special and treasured under his care and attention.

There were no problems during the drive to Goshen. I was filled with anticipation of my new life with Scott and knew that I could be happy with him anywhere. The drive had been long and uneventful with only the needed stops for gas and breaks. A fresh surge of excitement rushed through me and all fatigue vanished when the exit sign that would take me to Goshen appeared just ahead. I was immediately wide awake and alert. As I drove towards Goshen on that two lane highway, I tried to wrap my mind around the reality that these roads would soon be the routes I would travel in my daily life in Indiana. Everything looked different. The roads had numbers instead of names. Outside of town, every road looked the same with farmhouses and barns, totally different from the cities where I had lived and worked all my life. There were no landmarks at the four-way stops that connected these roads--only the occasional sign with an arrow pointing to the right or left for fresh produce of the season, fresh eggs, or a nursery. I was delighted with the mature blue spruce evergreen trees that were everywhere, planted as windbreaks on farms and also randomly scattered across the landscape. I could only imagine how beautiful they would look in winter with snow draped on their branches. A slow moving Amish buggy crossed the intersection at one four-way stop. Clotheslines adorned with dresses, pants, and shirts on the farms brought back memories of my own childhood when my sister and I hung the laundry outside and propped up the line with a notched cane fishing pole. Memories of shelling bushels of purple hull peas and butter beans on the front porch and picking blackberries with Aunt Lucy also flashed in my mind while I was driving. The road numbers were going down at each intersection, starting at 33 and counting down to CR 17. Scott and I had communicated throughout the day, with our conversations becoming more frequent, as the distance between us shortened. The last ten miles or so, we stayed on the phone until I pulled into his driveway where he was waiting with that beautiful smile. It was like our first meeting all over again.

We were inseparable during my first visit and every moment tingled with delight. He showed me his home in Bristol where he grew up and the places around town that he played as a kid with his friends. I hung onto every word, excited just to be with him for this short visit.

For our visit in June, he decided to fly down, instead of driving. I took him to the airport early on Monday morning for his return flight and went back home to get ready for work. I was preparing to leave when I heard a knock at the door. Scott was standing on the other side with that special twinkle in his eyes and the sweet smile I dearly loved. Naturally, I was surprised to see him. He explained that his flight had been delayed for a few hours. Rather than just sit at the airport, he had taken a cab back to my place, so we could enjoy breakfast together before I went to work. I was delighted and also amazed, as I lived about fifteen miles from the airport. When I asked about the cost of the cab, he waved it aside and said he had negotiated the fare. We had a wonderful breakfast at a local restaurant and then I took him back to the airport. I arrived late to work that day, but the memory was priceless.

Scott's words, dated 6/17/2007:

"You make every day special in my life. Your love has replaced the fear, the doubt, and the insecurity. My constant dream is to wake up with you every morning, to lie with you every night, to touch you every day. You've captured me completely, and I am yours totally."

I returned to Indiana for the week of the July fourth holiday. Scott had to work two of those days, so I spent one day with his mother. This was my first time to be alone with his mother, and I hoped I would leave her with a good impression at the end of the day. We visited the Shipshewana Flea Market, as well as some of the shops in town. Throughout the day, she shared details and stories about her and her spouse and their families. Scott had grown up with three older brothers and many cousins and extended family members involved in his life. He had a stable home environment and enjoyed many adventures growing up in a small town. Scott and I met up with his mom and dad the next evening for dinner, and I enjoyed watching him interact with his folks. It was very strange that after so many years and at my age, I would be subconsciously seeking the approval of a man's parents, and I was once again in awe of this major life change. I had a great time with Scott during this extended visit. He shared memories of younger days and his family. He talked about his brothers and school and life growing up in a small town. My love and admiration grew deeper, as he shared more about his past and himself.

Scott had determined that we would need a larger place to live in Goshen and had started looking for a house. He said the duplex where he lived was full of bad memories and unhappiness, and he did not want us to start our life together in that place. During my second visit to Goshen in July, Scott told me he had found a house for us, but he wanted me to see me it before he signed the lease. Touched that he cared about my opinion, I assured him that I trusted his judgment as he knew the area well; however, he insisted that I see the house first and called the leasing agent to arrange a viewing while I was in town. As Scott and I entered the front door, it finally registered that I was going to move to Goshen, that I was going to marry the man I loved, and that we were going to begin life together. Everything was falling into place all around me without any effort on my part. It was hard to leave Indiana after so many wonderful days with Scott, but as I drove south, I was aware of a new sense of purpose and direction. Once again, I was filled with reassurance about Scott's love, to trust it and receive it. My heart soared with joy in acceptance. Surely, I was the most blessed woman in the world.

I wanted my daughter to meet Scott, and we agreed that she would visit Goshen with me in August. My son was in the military and could not get leave at that time, but I knew he would trust whatever his sister shared with him about Scott. Our travel was uneventful and everything went smoothly. My daughter genuinely liked Scott. He was considerate of her and spent time talking to her one on one. She told me later that she respected the way he treated me and that his love and concern for me were obvious. She also met his parents, and Scott and I showed her around Elkhart County during this short, fun-filled visit.

Scott visited me in September, and we decided that October would be his last monthly visit in preparation for the move to Goshen in January. To save money, as the moving costs would be substantial, we would not travel in November or December. Scott would take care of all the moving arrangements and I would pack. He gave me one of my favorite cards during his visit in September that thrilled me inside and out! The plain card simply said, "I love you" on the front. On the inside, Scott had written these words from his heart:

"Iris,

My heart fills with joy when I imagine the day . . .

. . . The day we no longer say good morning with the tapping of the keyboard and the click of the mouse, but instead, a hug and a kiss.

. . . The day when our time apart is no longer measured with weeks and days, but with hours and minutes.

. . . The day we no longer say goodnight with the cold reminder of distance as we hang up the phone, but instead lying together, talking, touching, and the warm reminder of the love we share.

. . . The day we walk through the door of our home together, knowing we will never again be apart.

I love you, Iris!
Scott"

We celebrated my birthday on his last visit to my apartment the next month in October of 2007. After bringing in his bags, he went back outside to his truck. He was carrying an oversized present when he returned. Excitement was building, while I mentally tried to guess what was inside the wrapping paper. Scott was an excellent "gifter," always adding his own special touch. I was speechless as I gazed at the large, framed, double-matted print, titled "Oak Arches," with my own words printed in the bottom right hand corner. Scott had written a personal message on the back.

"I pray we walk many roads together with all the smiles and kisses your heart desires.

Love always,
Scott
October 19, 2007"

I sat there stunned and overwhelmed by the love behind this gift. I looked at Scott with tears in my eyes, thanking him repeatedly. He was unaware of the emotional whirlwind inside me, and I could not express my feelings adequately at that moment.

One afternoon, many months prior to meeting Scott, I was browsing on a website that sold posters and prints, looking at Black and White prints of trees. I love old trees, especially those with gnarly branches and age thickened trunks. One in particular spoke to me, titled "Oak Arches," with a row of mature oak trees forming a canopy over a dirt road leading to an unknown destination. I could not afford to make a purchase at that time, so I had printed a small thumbnail copy and push-pinned it to the bulletin board above my desk at work. During the days while I was working, my eyes drifted to that small image and different scenarios played out in my mind. One day while gazing at the small photo, the following words popped into my thoughts. I quickly jotted these down to post below the picture.

"Take my hand
walk with me
down the road
not knowing where
smile at me

kiss me
whisper my name
bliss."

I had looked at that image and my words for months and months.
Now, here I was holding an actual framed picture in my hands from this
wonderful man who wanted to walk with me down the same road. The
reality was breathtaking, and my heart flooded with love.

I had shared with Scott the story behind the "Oak Arches" photo after he had asked me to marry him in February. I had posted the details on
a blog at that time, and Scott commented in response, using his nickname for me, Rainbow:

"Rainbow posted the following poem on her April 19 blog. She sent
me a message explaining the history and meaning behind the poem.
Needless to say, I was deeply touched by both the poem and her message. To have the love of this amazing woman is a blessing from God.
Many have been touched by Rainbow's kind and caring nature, intelli-
gence, and boundless imagination, but to know all the colors and beauty
that make up this one-of-a-kind rainbow is truly an honor. I would love
to share with the world all of the excitement, joy, laughter, sensuality,
and love that Rainbow has given me in the time I have known her, but it
is all beyond mere words. Only God and I will know and fully appreciate
the blessing she has become in my life. I love her completely with
everything that I am and hope to one day take her hand and walk with
her down that road, not knowing where, but knowing we will get there
together.

Thank you, Darling, for your love.

Always and forever yours, Scott"

After Scott left for Indiana, my focus shifted to getting ready for the move. I spent my spare time sorting, donating, discarding, and packing. I brought home empty boxes from work, and rolls of packing tape and bubble wrap disappeared quickly into those boxes, as I carefully packed all of the breakables for safe travel to Goshen. I labeled each one and started stacking them in the spare bedroom. Funny how love can transform the most dreaded tasks into an exciting adventure. Occasionally, I would email updated pictures of the increasing number of boxes to show Scott my progress with the packing. Excitement grew with each box that I filled.

Posted by Scott 10/31/2007:

"I'm looking at the first card Rainbow sent to me in December of 2006 before we had met in person. This card is one of my most cherished possessions…in the event of a fire; I would grab my computer, coffee grinder, and this card.

It was the Christmas season for snail-mail and by no fault of her own; the card took forever to be delivered. Rainbow had been fretting the card would not make it before Christmas, but I was playing it cool…she has never known (until now) that I had been camped out by the mailbox for days in anticipation of its arrival. It finally arrived on December 23rd. We had been discussing the possibility of meeting in a public place over a cup of coffee…the card was perfect, one of the best Christmas gifts I had ever received…not only because of the card, but because I had something that had been written by her own hand, rather than tapped out on the keyboard. For some reason, that handwritten message meant so much to me; it was evidence that Rainbow was real, not just words on the monitor. It's the little things that bring so much joy.

The card now sits next to me on my desk. I often open the card, smile, and reminisce of how our story began.

Thank you Sweetheart for this beautiful gift."

Thanksgiving and Christmas of 2007 passed rather quickly. I spent time with my children, as my son was able to take leave for Christmas. We talked about this major life change and my move to Indiana at length. They were both happy for me, and I was thankful that they had a positive attitude about these changes. My daughter had obviously given her brother a favorable review of Scott after her visit to Indiana. Gratitude and love filled my heart.

Close to Christmas, I received a large package from Indiana at work. My mind was racing at the possible contents, and I waited until I arrived home that evening to open the box. There was a beautiful card inside with Scott's special handwritten words once again thrilling my heart. Excitedly, I opened the tissue covering and found a large plush red Christmas stocking. I was happily surprised. There was a key attached to the white cuff, and the stocking was full of wrapped gifts. Socks were draped over one side of the cuff. Tears bubbled up and spilled. I never had a stocking as a child and had hung my first stocking while I was married to my children's father.

After the divorce, it had seemed pointless to hang a stocking for myself at Christmas. Now, after all these years, I had received a stocking full of love. I was overwhelmed by Scott's thoughtfulness and care in selecting the gifts, wrapping each one, and packing the stocking and card for safe shipping. I opened each present stuffed inside the stocking, while talking to him on the phone. The conversation was as much fun as discovering the contents of the presents. He explained that the key belonged to his heart. Scott touched the deepest parts of my soul, he delighted me with his words and affection, and I was looking forward to spending every day with this wonderful man.

Scott made all the arrangements in advance. He drove a rental car to Memphis at the end of December, as he would be driving the moving truck back to Indiana, and I would follow him in my truck. The next morning, we picked up the twenty-six foot moving truck and drove it back to my place. We finished packing some odds and ends and set up the air mattress for the night. The moving company arrived on time the next day to load the truck. Everything went smoothly. I tried to sleep that night, but the reality of this life change was so strong, I could not quiet my mind, and it was early morning before I drifted off. When Scott woke me up, I felt like I had just closed my eyes.

After loading the last few items, I looked around at my empty apartment for the last time. This was the best apartment I had lived in since my divorce. All of the misery of the past years flashed by in a few seconds, followed by our meeting, the months of traveling and anticipation of our next short monthly visit, the emails and phone calls. Now Scott and I would be together from this day forward, and we would never have to say goodbye again. I looked at Scott, who was staying on task, totally unaware of my thoughts, and I thanked God for Scott's love and our new life.

We stopped at the leasing office to leave my keys in the drop box and drove out onto the highway. I looked around at my surroundings and knew I would not travel this way again, and I was filled with joy. I remembered that horrible night after I left the hotel room when I thought I would die, and instead I had received love. That realization remained in my mind throughout the trip to Indiana.

Chapter Three

THE LAND OF GOSHEN

We stopped only when necessary. Travel was slow with the large truck, and we both wanted to get home safely and not waste time during the drive. The weather was definitely colder as we neared Northern Indiana. About fifty miles from Goshen, the snow was falling softly. Night had descended, and now there was a renewed sense of urgency to get home. Scott was weary from the drive and maneuvering the truck through traffic and stops, and fatigue was beginning to settle into me as well from the lack of sleep the previous night. The familiar exit sign appeared in my headlights, and my heart jumped with excitement, as the memories of my first visit danced in my head. Refreshed, I enjoyed the final miles of the journey with the snow falling against the night sky. My thoughts circled around the blessings of love God had brought and the major life changes in a relatively short time. My future with Scott looked bright and secure.

We arrived safely. Most of the houses were dark on the street and only the lamp posts were glowing. Everyone was asleep, unaware of the great event taking place at our house. God had orchestrated our meeting and our relationship. He had guided us through the past year with love and reassurance, and now He had brought us to this home to continue growing in that love.

The movers arrived the next morning to unload, and then Scott and I returned the rental truck. The first thing Scott did was take me shopping for appropriate winter clothing and shoes, as my wardrobe was inadequate for this colder climate. I was incredibly happy at his concern for my health and safety. Within a few days, I had weatherproof shoes to keep my feet warm and dry, a much warmer winter coat, and appropriate gloves and socks.

So began our life together in Goshen--days of joy, peace, fun, laughter, and bliss. Life was in vivid color. We went everywhere and did everything together, holding hands walking across parking lots, hugging and smiling at each other often. I was thrilled to be with Scott, and he was proud to be with me. I marveled many times at this special man who had been walking around unattached before we met. Surely, I was not the only woman who could see the depth of Scott, his good qualities and strengths, his talents and abilities, besides his obvious physical attraction. Sometimes, I looked in the mirror and wondered what Scott saw when he looked at me, wishing that I could see myself through his eyes. Wonderful unexpected moments occurred randomly. Sudden mutual awareness would spring up between us, and we would stop what we were doing and look at each other at the same time. Scott would pull me close and ask me, "Where have you been all my life?" Smiling, I would touch his face in wonder and reply, "Where did you come from?" Though he was born in Bristol, Indiana, I truly believed part of Scott came from heaven. We knew God's hand was in all of this, and our love was special, powerful, and healing. We were in awe of Him, our love, and each other.

One evening we walked out onto the front porch with a fresh cup of hot coffee in hand. Night had fallen, and there was a slight chill in the air, as we settled into our chairs. Sipping our coffee in comfortable silence, my mind drifted back into the past. I had never known love like Scott and I shared and did not know this kind of love even existed. My first husband, the father of my children, had loved me as I had loved him, and he was a good father and provider, but our relationship was completely different. The lack of emotional intimacy between us spread into other areas of our marriage and after seventeen years, led him to seek affection/love elsewhere. He moved out in 1995, and the divorce was finalized in January of 1996. The years that followed were hellish. I lost everything that mattered to my heart. A part of me died when the dust finally settled and I was completely alone. I functioned on auto-pilot. The pain morphed into numbness, as life turned into bleak emptiness and extra work to make ends meet. A friend had suggested I needed to find someone to help me raise my children, but I had no interest in meeting anyone or dating. I paid my own way, working overtime, weekends, and holidays to cover living expenses, food, and basic needs, and I had sold the extra furniture and many things I had wanted to keep in order to live.

I had prayed when the father of my children left the home, but had no faith in my own prayers, and hoped against hope that maybe God would help me. I had not earned God's favor and doubted I would receive much help. I had felt insignificant in life from early childhood and had accepted that rejection as God's view of me. I was just another one of those throwaway kids who would never amount to anything. "Those poor girls don't stand a chance," I overheard someone say at a family gathering when I was a child, and I never forgot those words. The people at church treated me just like my family. I understood the church to be God's house and the people who attended to be God's people. In my young mind, if they rejected me, then God rejected me. I did not fit in with my family or the church people. I had never fit in anywhere and was constantly aware that I was different. That perception crippled me with fear and insecurity the majority of my life. I had loved hearing the Bible stories about Jesus and singing all the songs we learned in Sunday School in childhood. My father dropped my sister and me off at Sunday School and picked us up during the years we lived with him, and once we started living with Aunt Lucy, we rode the church bus to a local Baptist church every Sunday morning. I wanted to believe that Jesus loved all the children of the world, but I did not have parents like everyone else. Life was not normal while I was growing up. Something was wrong with me, because God did not love me as much as other children who did have parents and families. Now in my late 40's, God had brought a man into my life whose love far exceeded all my hopes and dreams. I was blessed to have a man I loved, respected, trusted, and desired deeply.

Scott took my hand, and we walked off the porch into the yard under the night sky. All the past hurt, anger, disappointment, betrayal, and resignation washed over me, as I stood hand in hand with this wonderful man. I did not understand why God had chosen to bless us so amazingly. Perhaps we had gone through enough heartache in our lives to earn some love and joy. Happiness and gratitude filled my heart, as I gazed up at the stars.

Chapter Four

LOVE TOUCHES

Scott touched the child in me and the hidden parts that I thought had died long ago. He gave me love and attention beyond what I had ever imagined or hoped to experience.

Scott and I were driving down a county road that we frequently traveled in our daily lives, and we passed a large modern bowling alley, Signature Lanes. More than twenty years had passed since I had bowled, and I suggested that we go bowling one night just for fun. Scott smiled and agreed, but did not commit to a specific night. The following weekend, we drove to Mishawaka for some shopping. Thoughts of my favorite stores were running through my mind during the drive, but Scott unexpectedly parked in front of a sporting goods store. Puzzled, I asked if we were looking for a gift, as we walked across the parking lot. He smiled at me and said, "We are here to buy bowling balls and bags." I was surprised and excited, as we entered the store, and we spent some time choosing the appropriate ball weight, color, and bags. We later carried the balls back to the bowling alley to be drilled, and I was fascinated by the whole process. It seemed like a lot of expense to play a few games, but Scott had a different mindset, and I followed his lead in expectation.

We bowled a few games, and he won every time. I felt uncoordinated watching him, as I had no form or confidence in my game. Scott graciously signed me up for lessons at the alley, and I appreciated his patience and desire for me to play well. He went with me on those nights, taking lessons as well from another instructor, and we bowled a few games afterwards. My confidence grew and my game improved, but in spite of my best efforts, Scott always beat my score. His competitiveness showed, and I teased him a little. He just said matter of fact, without arrogance or condescension, that he had bowled for years and played in leagues, and had won trophies in his younger years. He informed me that I was very competitive as well, though I would not admit it. I accepted his superior skill level, but continued to try to win. Those were fun nights. Everything felt special with Scott. On my birthday that year, he gave me a pair of blue bowling shoes--my first bowling ball, bag, and shoes.

Scott asked me to pick the month and date for our wedding, and I chose Saturday, October 4th. Fall is my favorite time of the year. I love the changing colors of the trees, the harvests of the season, the cool crisp nights, and the anticipation of the upcoming holidays. Though Fall had not officially started, and the weather can be unpredictable in Northern Indiana, we opted for a date early in the month. We elected to have an outdoor ceremony with our families present at the Essenhaus Covered Bridge in Middlebury, Indiana. Scott asked our pastor, Jim Brown, of Grace Community Church in Goshen, to officiate at our wedding, and we attended premarital counseling sessions with Pastor Brown in preparation for the special day.

Shopping for our wedding rings was a fun adventure, full of love and hope for our new life together. We had purchased them many weeks in advance and occasionally, I would take the rings out of the drawer and open the boxes in happy anticipation. Initially, I had chosen a plain gold band, but Scott had insisted that I needed some sparkle, and after a pleasant search, I found the perfect ring. The back of the band was solid white gold. The top of the band separated into three channeled bands. The two outside bands of yellow gold crossed in an "X" above the lower white gold band, which formed an oval "O". The "X" and "O" were filled with small diamond chips.

There was not a corresponding ring for the groom, but further searching produced a yellow and white gold band that appealed to Scott. Gazing at the ring on my finger, I reflected on how I had given up hope of love and marriage, and now I was making preparations to become a wife once again. I marveled at how God had changed my life so wonderfully, as I removed the ring and placed the box back in the drawer. Soon Scott would place the ring on my finger, and I would not have to take it off again.

We created our wedding announcement on the computer using a Fall scene with a large tree in full autumn splendor. He "drew" a heart on the tree trunk with the words "Scott and Iris" inside the heart and added special words to the details. Scott printed the announcements, as I addressed each envelope, and then we stuffed the envelopes together. The day was playful and full of promise for our shared life ahead.

Saturday was finally here. I was going to be Mrs. Scott Long before the day was over, and I was trying to process that as we were getting ready. My son and daughter arrived as well as Scott's daughter and her family, all from out of town. The remainder of his family would meet us in Middlebury. My best friend, Anita, and her husband, whose name was also Scott, traveled from Olive Branch, Mississippi, to attend the wedding, arriving in a rush of unexpected surprise early that afternoon. They had known me through the best and worst years, and I was touched by their loving kindness to make the trip and be a part of this incredible blessing. My head and heart were tumbling with emotion, happiness, tears, and joy, as the memories of all my yesterdays crashed into the reality of this day. The nervousness accelerated during the drive to Middlebury. Scott and I had chosen to repeat the traditional wedding vows, and fear that I would forget or misspeak some of the words was mounting.

Our wedding day was picture perfect. The afternoon sun was shining across the landscape, and the red covered bridge stood out strikingly against the bright blue sky. We stood under a tree on the bank of a small stream that trickled under the bridge. Large clumps of pampas grass adorned the gravel road at the bridge openings and swayed with a gentle breeze. I could hear the leaves rustling softly overhead. God seemed to be smiling down on us as we gathered together. Our pastor performed a beautiful ceremony, reading the scripture passages he had asked each of us to select, and praying over us and our marriage. Through all my tension and fear, I lost track momentarily during the ceremony. Suddenly aware of a pause, I mistook that moment of silence for the time that Scott was supposed to kiss the bride. Puzzled that he was not making a move towards me, I spoke out of turn and asked him if he was going to kiss me. He looked at me with such surprise that I knew I had misstepped, and I was instantly mortified. To save me any further embarrassment, Scott quickly kissed me, smiled at me, and stepped back into place. Our pastor just smiled and continued on with the service, prompting Scott to officially kiss me at the appropriate moment.

I was completely overwhelmed. I had resigned myself to a life of bleak survival, but God had lifted me out of that pit of self-condemnation and hopelessness to love me and to love Scott. Life had changed so quickly and so amazingly. I was deeply humbled by that realization once again and incredibly grateful, as Scott and I walked hand in hand as husband and wife for the first time.

Scott made a big deal out of my birthday. Another present in 2008 was a large square box, wrapped very prettily. He had already proven that he gave the best presents, and I could not guess what this box contained. Unwrapping the tissue paper inside, I found a set of six hand-painted iris plates. Questions gushed out in delighted confusion...How did he get these? When did he buy them? During Scott's first visit, I had taken him to the antique mall, where I'd had a booth for four years, to introduce him to the other vendors and to show him the building. Junk-ing, as I called it, had given me something to do on weekends when I was not working and had kept my mind and hands busy. I enjoyed setting up displays in my booth and maintaining the appeal of my small space. Scott was impressed with the market, because it was all vintage or antique merchandise, with no imports or mass produced items. One of the vendors and her husband cleaned out estate sales, requiring several booths for all their wares. As Scott and I were browsing through this area, I had spotted a set of iris plates. Though not a plate collector, the oval shape and the colors of the flowers were very appealing. The cost for all six was more than I wanted to spend, even priced at a discount.

In February of 2007, the owner of the building had informed the vendors that due to health problems with her husband and mother she was going to have to close the market after ten years of business. She could no longer take care of her family and maintain the business, as it was open every day of the week and she had to drive some distance back and forth from home. I slashed prices in my booth, as did the other vendors, to sell off as much as possible before the first of April. When Scott visited in March, he offered to help me pack up what was left. He went a step further and loaded all the boxes and a few tables in his truck to take back to Indiana, as that would be less to move later. He was already thinking ahead! We walked through the market for the last time, and I looked for those plates hoping for a deeper discount; however, they had already sold. Now, I was looking at Scott with a big question mark on my face, as I held the plates in my hand. With a sweet smile, Scott explained that he had stopped at the market on his trip back to Indiana after our visit in March and had bought the plates. He asked the owner and the other vendors not to tell me, as he was going to surprise me with them later. He had brought the plates home and hid them away, until my first birthday in Indiana. I was once again stunned by his thoughtfulness and desire to make me happy.

We were very excited for our first Christmas together and spent many hours searching for the perfect tree. We agreed on an artificial tree, as we had carpet and wanted to decorate it Thanksgiving weekend. We shared our childhood Christmas memories as we shopped. Scott's family decorated a real tree every Christmas during his childhood, and I had enjoyed a real tree for a few years in my twenties during my first marriage.

One Saturday, we drove out to Eby's Evergreen Plantation where Scott and his family had gone in years past. He surprised me when he asked if I would like to choose a tree and suggested that we set it up outside in the front yard and decorate it with lights and weatherproof ornaments. I was delighted with the idea. We drove onto the tree farm, taking a saw provided at the gate, and set off in search of a tree. This was my first experience on a tree farm, and I was moving from one tree to the next, circling around the possibilities, trying to find the one that was perfect on all sides. After checking out another section, I found the tree. It was symmetrical and full with outswept branches that would display the lights gloriously. Scott had to get on the ground to cut it down, as the branches were low on the trunk. As we picked it up to load it on the truck, I felt a twinge that perhaps the tree was a little oversized. Even with the tailgate down, the tree extended beyond the edge and the lower trunk was very large in diameter. It must have measured at least ten feet tall. We returned the saw and after the tree was shaken and netted, we headed home.

Setting the tree proved to be somewhat of a challenge. Scott used a heavy duty stand suitable for outdoors and also staked the tree. We spent the rest of the evening decorating the tree, using a tall stepladder to drape the lights and secure them to the branches. When we finally stood back to admire our efforts, the tree looked magical. The round clear lights were shining brightly in the dark night and my heart was soaring. I was once again in awe of Scott and his ability to surprise me and delight me beyond my wildest dreams.

While browsing through the Christmas decorations in a local store, Scott spotted some red, white, and green bead garland with bells attached. Jingling the bells, he smiled and asked me if I would like a jingle bell curtain for the office door. I worked full-time at home and we used the third bedroom as an office. We both had a desk and a computer in the room. Although Scott worked in an office, sometimes he needed to work on projects at home in the evening. The office door always remained open, and Scott's idea sounded like something fun to enjoy through the season. Intrigued, I watched him string the garland into rows using a tension rod, until it was full enough to be a curtain. He mounted it in the doorway of the office and I was surprised at how much I liked it. He was happy that I appreciated his efforts. The bells jingling every time one of us walked through made me smile, and the sound touched something in my heart. Scott knew how to connect with me in simple, yet profound ways. We did silly and fun together, and it was wonderful.

One of the many gifts I received from Scott that Christmas, which impressed me greatly, was a large gift set of Tresor. The name was familiar, but I had never worn that fragrance. Sniffing the bottle, I thought the fragrance was slightly heavy. Careful not to display any disappointment, I held my initial opinion to myself, while I applied a few dabs to my skin. A short while later, Scott asked what I thought of the scent. As I lifted my wrist to my nose, I was very pleasantly surprised, because the fragrance had mellowed and smelled divine. I happily encouraged Scott to give me his opinion, as I extended my wrist towards him. He smiled and confirmed the fragrance was a perfect match for me. At that moment, I had the strangest impression that he already knew it would be when he purchased the set. But how did he know? I felt like a princess wearing this expensive fragrance, and the set included lotion and body powder, which I love. No one had ever selected a perfume for me, and I felt incredibly special every time I wore this fragrance. He gave me a Christmas card with his personal message written inside, and I treasured these special words from his heart:

"My Dear Iris,

I am so grateful we're together this Christmas. This is just the first of many special Christmas Days we'll share. You are wonderful and I'm so blessed to have you for my wife.

I love you with all my heart baby!

Merry Christmas!

Love always,
Scott"

I had shared with Scott one favorite childhood memory was Aunt Lucy's fried chicken, which she sometimes cooked on Sundays after church. She fried the chicken in a deep cast iron skillet using another skillet as a lid. After frying the chicken, she saved part of the drippings to make milk gravy for the biscuits. Scott surprised me when he said that he wanted us to cook the same meal. I explained I had not eaten a chicken dinner like that in many years, and that a large deep cast iron skillet would be expensive and I was not sure how often we would use it. Scott, however, was not concerned about the cost and was ready to start this adventure. We drove to a store in Warsaw that sold cast iron and found the skillet. We stopped at a grocery store on the way back home for the chicken and all the fixings for our dinner. Scott watched as I prepared the food and served the meal. I was taken back to those Sunday dinners when I was a young teen. I was not sure why Scott wanted to do this, but I really enjoyed our dinner that night. Not to be outdone, Scott later announced that he was going to prepare the next chicken dinner in the cast iron skillet. I knew instinctively that he had been searching recipes on the Internet, and I challenged him to outshine my efforts. To Scott's credit, his chicken dinner was delicious. Again, I was overwhelmed by his kindness and commitment to my happiness. His devotion touched me in a way I did not understand. His father, at a later time, explained that Scott had simply wanted to experience that same dinner with me, because it was special to me.

My houseplants were the last to be loaded onto the moving truck before the drive to Goshen. I had three very large plants that needed to be repotted before the Spring of 2008. Scott moved the heavy pots to the garage and helped me transplant the overgrown plants into larger planters. It was an arduous task and I was thankful he was willing to help me. I had brought a wooden bench when I moved to Goshen and used this for the large green plants, which I would transfer to the porch once Spring arrived. His roll-around mechanic's stool in the garage made the repotting easier. Our flower beds had been previously landscaped with bushes and rocks, so I planned to mount flower boxes on the porch railing and place decorative pots on the porch and steps. Spring arrived much later in Goshen than I was accustomed to in the South, and I was impatiently waiting for signs of new life outside. The garden centers had begun to stock flowers and plants in April, but I had been advised by many locals not to plant anything until after Mother's Day. Scott traveled with me to different nurseries to search for the best plants the weekend before the holiday and mounted the brackets for the window boxes on the railing. I was eager to plant the flowers and add some color and charm to the front of our home.

The Sunday before Mother's Day, after attending church, Scott suggested we spend a lazy afternoon around the house. We did some chores together, and then Scott said he was going to work in the garage a while. He asked me not to come out there, as he did not want any distractions. The garage was cold, and I had some things I could do in the house in the meantime. After a bit, he came inside and said he had something to show me in the garage. Just as I started to open the door, he instructed me to close my eyes. He then took my hand and guided me through the door and down the steps. I could not begin to guess what he was up to. I assumed that he had been working on organizing his workbench and the garage and probably wanted me to admire the results.

Anticipation was building, and I was more than a little excited. Finally, he stopped and told me to open my eyes. I gasped in surprise. I was standing in front of a full size potting bench and a watering hose cart. He explained that he had watched me while I was working with the houseplants and thought this bench would make it easier for me to plant my flowers. The bench had been shipped to his work address earlier in the week. While I was working inside the house, he had been in the garage assembling the bench. The hose cart would allow me to connect the hose outside, enabling me to water all the flowers and plants much easier than multiple trips with a watering can. He showed me how to connect/disconnect the hose to the outside faucet and to rewind the hose on the drum--a vast improvement. The cart could then be rolled back into the garage. Tears welled up and spilled over at his thoughtfulness and concern for what I enjoyed. Again, he had touched the deepest part of me with more love than I could comprehend. He connected with my soul.

Scott continued to amaze me, watching how I performed tasks and then changing something to make work easier. We had recently bought matching desks for our home office. The desks had a center drawer just wide enough for a keyboard and a mouse, but not much room to move the mouse. We were both working at home one evening, and he surprised me a few days later with a nice keyboard mount. He removed my desk drawer, mounted the platform, and set up the keyboard and mouse. He explained that he had watched me struggle to use my mouse with the drawer and thought this would help me work more efficiently. He had shelves made for my office paraphernalia and pictures so I could unpack those and have them around me as I worked. Again, I was filled with appreciation for this man and his love. His kindness and thoughtfulness were limitless.

My birthday was coming up after our anniversary in 2009, and I was wondering if Scott was planning anything special. Not that he needed to; his words in a card were enough, but I had come to understand that Scott really enjoyed doing things that would make me happy. The Friday before my birthday, Scott called and suggested that we eat dinner at our favorite restaurant in Goshen. I changed clothes and was ready when he came by and picked me up after work. We had just been served our beverages when my daughter walked up to our table. I squealed when I saw her, and she started laughing at my surprise. Scott had arranged in advance for her to travel from Memphis to celebrate my birthday with us. We enjoyed our dinner, as they filled me in on the arrangements made in secrecy. Once we arrived home and I was settled in a chair, Scott and my daughter proceeded to ad lib a game show scenario. I wondered if they had planned this part, too. They were in sync with one another with their presentation, and I was laughing at their antics.

Scott was holding three large clasp envelopes. For my birthday, I had the choice of watching T.V. and playing a computer game all weekend, or I could have the prize inside one of the three envelopes. I thought they must be clowning around, but Scott assured me I would receive the contents of any envelope I chose. Excitement escalated as I made my selection and eagerly watched Scott open the envelope. He pulled out a printed placard for a trip to Bronner's Christmas Wonderland in Frankenmuth, Michigan, including a hotel stay at the Bavarian Inn and their famous chicken dinner, plus spending money to shop at Bronner's. OH MY! WOW!!! He had completely blown me away with this surprise.

After moving to Goshen, I had spent some time searching the Internet for places of interest in our general area. I had found Bronner's and wanted to go, as it was hailed as the "World's Largest CHRISTmas Store" in the country! Scott was less enthusiastic when I sent him a link, pointing out that it was close to a five hour drive. Sensing his disinterest, I had not mentioned it again and the idea had faded. I could not speak at first, as I realized he must have been planning this trip for a while, and I had no clue. I jumped up out of my chair in delight and hugged him and kissed him and hugged my daughter, and we all laughed at my reaction. Then, curious, I asked about the other prizes. With that special twinkle in his eyes and mischievous smile, he handed me the other two envelopes. Secretly, I was wondering if something better could be in one of the other envelopes, and I laughed as I opened them, as they both contained the same prize!!! We all laughed and I cried a little, as I had not expected such a birthday celebration. He gave my daughter spending money, also, in a separate envelope. My heart was overflowing with his generosity and love towards my daughter and how blessed I was through this man's heart.

On October 20, 2009, I posted on Scott's social media page, "Thank you for loving me so much". He replied, "It's my favorite thing to do!"

Prior to Thanksgiving, we drove to nearby Syracuse, Indiana, to visit a store that sold close-out furniture and home decor. We had recently bought a large rug and a chair to accent our sofa, and we needed one more chair to complete the seating area. I found the perfect wing chair at this shop. The fabric and style immediately grabbed my attention. Even better, the price had been reduced two times and was very affordable. Christmas was on the horizon, however, and I was hesitant about the purchase, because we had not started shopping yet for the holiday. This would be a large purchase for us, and after much silent deliberation while browsing around the store a few times, I decided to hold off on the chair.

Close to Christmas Eve, Scott came home from work one day at lunch and drove my vehicle back to work. He said he needed to pick up something that he did not want to load in the back of his truck. Later that evening when he arrived home, he asked me to stay in the office and close the door until he called my name. After several minutes, he opened the door like nothing unusual had happened. I walked into the kitchen to start dinner and stopped in my tracks. In the great room, positioned by the Christmas tree, was a large sheet covered piece of furniture with a sign attached that read, "No Peeking." Laughing with delighted surprise, I listened as Scott explained that he had driven over to the shop one day after our visit, and a sign was posted on the door, "Closed for the Season." Apparently, there was a phone number listed on the sign, because Scott contacted the owner who agreed to meet him at the store to purchase the chair. He never ceased to amaze me with his love and desire to see me happy. How could anyone love me so much? Surely, I did not deserve this much love and attention.

There were many special moments and delightful surprises over the next year, and life was very good. We continued to attend church regularly and to spend time with our families. We remained in awe of our meeting and love and marriage. God had brought a man into my life and heart that I could share myself with completely, openly and honestly, without fear of rejection. The trust and respect were mutual. Every minute was good, whether shared in comfortable silence, working on tasks, fun excursions, or breathless moments. I thanked God every day for the love of Scott and our life together.

Chapter Five

MOVE TO HEAVEN

I did not know the evening of March 21, 2011 would be our last night together. It was a typical Monday evening, and we went to bed at our usual bedtime at 11:00pm. We watched T.V. for about twenty minutes, and then I turned it off. I heard Scott snoring softly, as I drifted off to sleep. Prior to 3 a.m. something woke me. The room was eerily quiet. Even with the hum of the ceiling fan and the sound machine, I could feel the silence. I sat up in bed and called out Scott's name, with no answer. I reached over, gently nudged him, and said his name again a little louder, with no answer. I jumped out of bed and turned on the light, calling his name even louder, with no answer. He was lying in the same position as when we went to bed. His eyes were closed and lips were slightly parted. The covers were not disturbed. Shaking him harder, I shouted his name, again with no response, and I dialed 9-1-1. The operator walked me through mouth-to-mouth. I breathed repeatedly into my husband's cold lips and each time, there was only a horrible gurgling sound in response. I started chest compression and counted out loud into the phone, until the paramedics arrived. Mentally, I was begging God, "Please don't take him, Please don't take him, Please don't take him." I continued to pray on the ride to the hospital, unable to believe he was gone. I asked the policeman who was driving me to the hospital behind the ambulance to please call our pastor and Scott's employer for prayer coverage. I gave him their names and silently continued to pray. There was no answer at the pastor's number, but Scott's employer and his wife said they would come to the hospital.

I walked into the emergency room entrance in numb shock. I was given an option to wait in the chapel room or the waiting room. I opted for the chapel. The woman at the desk was very helpful. She asked if I wanted her to call anyone. I asked her to call Scott's parents and brothers, but I could not talk to them. I could not think. I could not accept this reality. A detective positioned a chair in front of me and began to question me about the details leading up to the 9-1-1 call, after turning on a recorder and setting it on the table next to us. I answered his questions with surreal composure, completely numb. I sat there in disbelief, unable to process beyond the moment. I did not want to see tomorrow and the next day and the next day without Scott. It took all my strength and focus just to sit there and breathe. Scott's employer and his wife, followed by his parents and family arrived at that time. When those familiar faces walked in, I broke down and cried out, "He's gone, he's gone" through my sobs. I hugged them all, as I recounted what had happened.

The ER doctor came into the chapel and asked the family to come back to the room where they had taken Scott. He explained that they had tried everything, and there was no response to any resuscitative measures. The doctor was going to have to pronounce him dead. I had believed with vague hope that Scott would be revived once the ambulance arrived at the hospital. I looked over at his body on that table in silent horror. I walked over to him and ran my fingers through his hair. When we watched T.V., Scott loved to lay his head in my lap, while I massaged his scalp and played with his hair. Memories flashed as I stroked his hair for the last time. In that moment, I realized that Scott was gone before he was ever placed in the ambulance, before I called 9-1-1, before I was awakened. The body lying lifeless on the table was only a shell, because Scott had moved to heaven.

It was later determined that Scott had been dead about an hour to an hour and a half when the paramedics arrived. An autopsy was performed, because he had no medical history and he was only 44 years old. The coroner ruled that he died of natural causes due to congestive heart failure, secondary to a cardiomyopathy from a remote viral illness. He did not have a heart attack or suffer a stroke; rather, his heart just stopped beating. I was stunned at his diagnosis. He had never exhibited any signs or symptoms of congestive heart failure. We had been very active over the weekend, and he had not voiced any complaints, other than congested sinuses. It did not seem possible that he could die without being sick beforehand. Once I received the autopsy report, I shared copies with Scott's parents and brothers. He had left this world quietly, suddenly, without warning, without outward illness, while his body had been sick on the inside. I had to give that pain to God, as I could not bear it alone.

Scott had departed this earth in silence, and someone had awakened me shortly after his departure. He left for work much earlier than I started on my job, and every morning without fail, Scott kissed me goodbye before he left the house. Had he awakened me with a last kiss goodbye, or had an angel awakened me? Many months later, after reflection and revelation, I thanked God for His mercy in waking me early, so that I did not sleep next to his dead body for hours before awakening.

Scott's mother and his oldest brother's wife drove me home from the hospital and stayed at the house. Other family members arrived and gathered in the kitchen and great room, while I went to the bedroom to lie down. I could hear the flow of their conversation and laughter. Meanwhile, my heart was broken and my mind felt paralyzed. Suddenly, the alarm clock sounded at the appointed time for Scott to arise and get ready for work. In shock, I hurried to shut off the blaring reminder that Scott was gone.

The representative from the funeral home came by later in the morning to write the obituary and finalize funeral preparations. Scott's mother and daughter, who had just arrived, provided pertinent information. Pastor Jeremiah Olson, the worship pastor from Grace Community Church who would be officiating at Scott's funeral, came by as well. I shared details of our meeting, my move to Goshen, and our marriage. Scott's mother provided childhood memories and family stories.

Scott's daughter told us that she had never seen her father as happy as he had been during his years with me. His mother confirmed that same observation and shared that he had withdrawn from family gatherings and his visits were very short prior to meeting me. I had not known those details, as I had only known Scott as happy. We had attended all of the family gatherings together and stayed for hours at those visits. His family had noticed this change in Scott's attitude and behavior after he met me. I was happy to hear how much our love had impacted Scott, though bittersweet at this point.

Choosing his clothing for burial was surreal. I pulled out the suit he had worn to his daughter's wedding the year prior to our marriage and remembered the pictures of different shirts and ties he had emailed for my opinion prior to making a decision. I ran my hand lovingly over the shirt he had chosen and the corresponding tie. Memories of other shopping trips flooded over me, and the tears flowed, as I gathered the clothing for the funeral home.

I rode with the sister-in-law and Scott's mother to the funeral home to drop off his suit and onto the florist to select the casket floral spray. Lost in my thoughts in the back seat, I was barely aware of the conversation up front. Scott's sister-in-law was tense, as we drove to the funeral home. She shared that his oldest brother was angry that Scott had died and left me with the family. Her hurtful words stabbed my heart and a heavy silence filled the car.

I was half alive and half dead. Part of my heart was missing, and I did not know how to function without it. My children were traveling to Goshen for the funeral and would stay with me several days afterwards. My son was driving from Rapid City and would arrive early the next morning. My daughter was flying into South Bend and would arrive around 9:30 p.m. I knew the route to the airport from the 20 Bypass, but on this particular night, a section of the bypass was closed that included the airport exit. Traffic was redirected to a different exit into an unfamiliar area. I tried to remain calm, as I followed the orange detour sign. Rain had started falling and it was now 9 p.m. I drove about ten minutes along this route, until I realized I was not traveling in the direction of the airport. I stopped at a fast food restaurant and spotted a large family group seated inside. I asked them for directions for an alternate route to the airport. They instructed me to go to the bypass and take the airport exit. I tried unsuccessfully to explain the road situation; however, they were apparently unaware of the bypass closing and insisted that was the route I needed to follow. Exasperated, I thanked them and drove on further, stopping at Culver's, another fast food restaurant. The manager was not sure of the location of the airport, but offered to search an internet map. She kindly printed off the directions to the airport, and I sat in my car trying to get my bearings. I was still carrying the mobile phone Scott had purchased before I moved to Goshen, and my daughter called at 9:30. She had landed safely. I explained the situation to her and reassured her I would be there soon. Urgency and desperation were rising, as I read the map instructions. I did not recognize the street names. I called my in-laws and they suggested I call Scott's brother who lived in South Bend for help, as they were not familiar with the area. He was able to direct me to the local street to the airport, and I thanked him through the tears that had begun to fall. As I drove further along this street, an orange detour sign loomed through my headlights in the now pouring rain, redirecting me through another unfamiliar neighborhood. At this point, I yelled out in frustration, fear, and anger, asking God to please help me and to protect my daughter, until I could find the airport. Thankfully, this was a simple detour and I was able to get back on the main road without any mishap. By the time I arrived at the airport, it was after 10:30 p.m. I smiled in tearful gratitude when I saw my daughter sitting patiently on a bench. I hugged her tightly in relief and love.

There were many people who came to Scott's funeral that I did not know. I was introduced to a few of the unfamiliar faces, but many remained a blur. The service was comforting in spite of the pain, and Pastor Jeremiah's words were reassuring. After his opening remarks and prayer, he stated what all of us were thinking as we sat together in painful silence, "We weren't supposed to be here today. This doesn't feel right, this doesn't seem right." A deep sigh escaped from within at his words, relieved that he understood and shared our pain. Pastor Jeremiah spoke of our love story and Scott's childhood. Honor and pride filled my heart, as he talked about Scott's character and reputation. He then read the scripture passage that Scott had chosen for our wedding:

"Therefore, as God's chosen people, holy and dearly loved, clothe yourselves with compassion, kindness, humility, gentleness and patience. Bear with each other and forgive one another if any of you has a grievance against someone. Forgive as the Lord forgave you. And over all these virtues put on love, which binds them all together in perfect unity." (Colossians 3:12-14 NIV)

Scott's employer, Chris, who was also his spiritual mentor and friend, spoke at the service and shared a humorous glimpse into their relationship. I smiled as I listened to his words, thankful that the respect and affection Scott held for his boss was mutual. Pastor Jeremiah shared the role Chris had played in Scott's salvation. During a dark period in Scott's life, Chris had ministered to him and invited him to church. He was present when Scott went forward for salvation and received a snowflake token on that life-changing day. I had known that Scott was saved before I met him, but he had not shared the specifics, and I smiled in spite of the pain upon hearing these extra details. There were two readings as well, and then Scott's oldest brother spoke.

All of the employees at Team Construction Company, where Scott worked as a draftsman, came to the visitation and attended the funeral service. One of the men brought the picture that Scott had kept of me on his desk and placed it in the casket. The next day, I brought the original thumbnail picture of "Oak Arches," which I had kept in my desk after Scott gave me the large print, and tucked it inside the frame before the funeral. At the end of the funeral service, Scott's brothers walked to the casket together and placed a GI Joe into the casket, as all four brothers had played with GI Joes as kids. His family had not informed me that they were planning to do this, but I knew Scott would understand their behavior.

Loss and pain and questions filled my heart, as I rode mindlessly to the cemetery. Scott's parents had graciously acquired the burial plots, and his body was laid to rest under a grand old tree. As I listened to the prayer at the burial site, it seemed that all of the love and happiness Scott and I had experienced had disappeared into the grave as well. The family regrouped at Grace Community Church after the service, which had kindly provided food for all of us. Walking into the church without Scott took my breath away. I had always attended with him, and now his family and I were eating a meal together here at our church without him. His family returned to their own lives and I went to our house alone with my children. The finality of death hit home.

The house was quiet and empty without Scott. I wandered slowly through the rooms of our home. I walked into our bathroom and picked up his toothbrush. He would never use it or his hairbrush or his razor again. His slippers were waiting for him in their usual spot. Everything looked the same, but nothing was the same. Life was changing once again.

TRIBUTE TO SCOTT

"My deepest, heartfelt thanks to all of you who offered comforting words to me and my family following the passing of my baby brother, Scott. I have been to many viewings and funerals in my day and never thought my presence could make even a tiny difference to a family going through such a mind numbing event. Why even go? What could I say that that could possibly give any comfort whatsoever? Come tomorrow morning, they won't even know I was there... I was so wrong! Every single one of you made a huge difference.

Every tear shed, every hug, every handshake, every Facebook comment, every memory shared, every sympathy offered, and even every look of sympathy from a complete stranger from across the room, as our eyes met for a split second, was like a tiny steel thread that helped to stitch back together a family's heart that had been ripped to shreds. Our family is now closer than ever before, and I hope it stays this way.

As I watched the sun come up this morning, it dawned on me (pun intended) that there is more love in this world than I was ever remotely aware of, both incoming and outgoing. I am not done crying yet, but amazingly, I often find them to be tears of gratitude and joy, along with those of sorrow and grief. We always wonder "why" when something like this happens, and what lesson or purpose there could possibly be in something so horrible. Maybe this is it...to awaken the love that's in our hearts, both for the one lost, as well as for those around us. Thank you all so very, very much.

Scott David Long...by his death, he was increased." – Mike Long

Chapter Six

LIFE WITHOUT SCOTT

Within a few days of Scott's departure, I received a large envelope in the mail. A member of Scott's extended family sent a letter and information about grief, along with a check and some scriptures and prayers. She explained that she had been married to a pastor in another lifetime and wanted to send me some information that would be of help. I needed to be aware that I was emotionally vulnerable, because of this loss, and spiritually, the enemy would try to come into my thoughts and emotions. She enclosed a prayer, instructing me to stand in each room of the house and recite the prayer out loud. Even though it might feel strange doing so, she emphasized that I needed to do this in every room including closets, basement, and garage. She said if at a later time I felt that something was not right in the house, to repeat the prayer in each room.

This spiritual guidance came just as I needed it. Condemning thoughts had already started in my head. I must have done something wrong for God to take Scott, or Scott must have done something wrong. We had displeased God in some way, and death was the punishment. The scriptures she enclosed disproved these thoughts, and I read them over many times. I also listened to ministries on radio and T.V., and I read multiple faith-based books on grief, loss, and healing, in search of comfort and godly counsel. To help take the focus off of my own crushing pain, I read the obituaries in the local paper and prayed for the families and friends of those strangers over the loss of their loved ones. I reminded myself that other people were hurting and crying just like me, with the same kind of pain and hopelessness that I was experiencing.

I prayed often throughout the days and nights and talked to God through the tears, crying until my tears ran dry. Memories with Scott constantly filled my mind and heart. The first two nights, I believed an angel would come and take me, too. Surely, God was not going to leave me here alone. I continued to relive our last night together, and all I could see was the body lying in our bed. I cried out and asked God to please have mercy that I did not want to keep seeing that image of Scott, and to bring back the happy memories. The next night, I was relieved that those death images were absent. I moved over to Scott's side of the bed and slept peacefully throughout the night, thankful for the blessing of rest. I had no appetite and forced myself to eat a little something at least once a day.

I resumed working the next week. Scott and I had signed into Instant Messenger every workday and exchanged a few messages throughout the day. Now, there was no reason to sign in, as there would be no response on the other end. Scott typically came home for lunch, as we lived close to his place of employment. I would greet him in the kitchen after hearing him enter the house through the garage. When he arrived home at the end of the day, he would open the door with a hearty, "Hey babe!" I would never hear his voice again. There would be no more handwritten notes or cards, no smiles, no hugs or kisses, no coming home.

I continued to attend our same church alone. The next Sunday, I drove to church with a heavy heart. Walking into the door without Scott was incredibly painful. He always opened the door and smiled at me, as he waited for me to walk through. Just seven days ago, he had sat beside me, and we had enjoyed our day with no warning that he would be leaving soon. I was tempted to stay home and avoid people, but God prompted me to continue in church for the spiritual nourishment. I needed the truth of God's Word and the insights provided by the pastor's messages, to continue to grow and develop in my relationship with God. That anchor would strengthen me and provide spiritual stability in my life. I had not attended any church regularly since my childhood, until I moved to Goshen with Scott. Now, more than ever, I needed to attend faithfully.

I had been carrying a newer and smaller Bible to church, but after Scott's move to heaven, I wanted to use the Women's Devotional Bible that my friend, Anita, had given me in September of 2000. When she gave it to me, I was more interested in the devotions than in reading the corresponding scriptures. She had written her favorite passage inside the Bible cover, Matthew 6:25-34, and I reread those verses many times. There was love associated with this Bible from the giver that I needed as well.

The week following the funeral, I received a call from a woman whose husband had worked with Scott. She called to check on me and asked if I would like to meet her for coffee next week at "The Electric Brew," a local coffee house in Downtown Goshen. I was very surprised at her call and a little excited to have a plan. When Scott died, all plans ended--no more weekend plans, holiday plans, or vacation plans. Now, I had a single plan to write on the calendar besides church on Sundays. A little spark lighted inside. I had also received many cards through the mail and messages via email and on social media, and every single one felt like a hug from God, a thread of hope for the future, encouraging words, prayers for my healing, to let me know people were thinking of me.

I was isolated in Goshen without Scott, as I had no personal friends locally or at church. We had attended regularly and had supported the church, but had not served or become more involved. We were only married 2-1/2 years and were still on our honeymoon at the time of his death. His family was dealing with their grief in their own way, and my children lived a long distance away. I began to see that God was ministering to me through these other means, and I thanked Him for every touch I received. I asked Him to bless those who had been kind to me and had prayed for me and who were thinking of me with love. My neighbors were concerned about me, and they stopped by to check on me from time to time. Some of them had brought food over when Scott died, and they continued to interact with me through the following months. I felt reassured that there was help close by should I need any assistance.

My first meeting with Sue at "The Electric Brew" was on Tuesday, April 5, 2011. My spirits were lifted as I left the house for this social visit. I had only seen her twice before at the annual Christmas party hosted by Scott's employer, and we had not engaged in personal conversation at those times. She was caring and concerned, and I felt at ease with her at our first meeting. She listened as I cried and talked about Scott, our marriage, and his death and she prayed for me at the end of our visit. We planned to meet the next week at the same time, same place, and we continued to meet over the next few months. The time I spent with her was a special gift, and I called her "Angel Sue". God knew I needed to talk to someone besides Him, and He sent a faithful servant who said yes to His call. I believe He only sent one person to me at that time, so that I would not be distracted from the Source of my help. I was aware that God was with me, and even during the most painful moments and gut wrenching cries, a sweet peace filled my soul. I realized that I was not walking alone through this dark valley. The tears continued to fall while I was learning and growing in my relationship with God through this pain.

Sue shared with me that her mother was a widow and talked about her mother's grief following the death of her father. She loaned me two books to read that her mother had written about her life and marriage. The second book included her grief journal, and some of those entries expressed the same questions and thoughts I was experiencing. The words were very healing and reassuring, strengthening and encouraging me during that time.

I wanted Scott's daughter and brothers to have some mementos of his life from the years they had shared. I returned Scott's boyhood baseball uniforms to his mother, as well as pictures from his past prior to our meeting. He had saved the large metal Tonka trucks from his childhood, and I gave those to his daughter for his grandchildren, as well as the GI Joes he had collected over the years. Each brother was allowed to choose one from the collection for themselves, and his daughter took the remainder. The brothers took the special baseball he kept on his desk from his childhood, his glove, and different trophies and keepsakes from younger years. Scott's oldest brother thanked me for loving his brother and making him happy.

Scott was the youngest of four brothers, and it did not make sense that he had died first at such a young age. He was loved and happy when he moved to heaven, after living unhappy and unfulfilled in different ways for many years. Now, after less than three years of marriage, his life on earth was over. I prayed that God would continue to walk with each of his brothers and his daughter through their individual grief journeys.

On May 3, 2011, I received a very special hug from God in the mail. The envelope contained a handwritten letter with a list of names and addresses, as well as a check and a game card. I played a farm game on Facebook and had become friends with some of the game neighbors.

"Dearest Iris,

It is with great love that we present you with this check for $405. You are free to use the money however you wish. We suggest you consider airfare to visit family, a massage or facial, or a couple of nights at a favorite hotel. Of course, we also expect that you have bills that need to be paid.

After Scott passed, Peggy and I were discussing our desire to be millionaires. We wished we could send you a ticket to visit us in Colorado-- we would go to a swanky resort and live like queens for a week.

Sadly, we are not millionaires and twenty dollars won't go far in easing your pain or helping you.

BUT!...you have a lot of Facebook friends and those friends have been pouring out their hearts with love and sympathy...I bet THEY have twenty bucks!

Iris, you need to know how excited these women were to help you. Maureen's young daughter overheard what we were doing and she chipped in, too! Some of us were only able to give $10, but others sent $50. Everyone sent love and support and prayers.

We love you, Iris, and we know you will live strong.
With much love and best wishes,
Your Facebook friends"

I was completely overwhelmed as I read and reread the letter. I looked at the check and the game card in disbelief. I thanked God over and over for this love and affection from across many, many miles. The return addresses from these friends covered different states including Texas, Colorado, Florida, Pennsylvania, Massachusetts, and New York. I prayed and asked Him to bless each person in a special way as I wrote and mailed thank you cards to every name on the list.

Journal entry dated 5/21/2011:

I went to the store late this afternoon to get some coffee. On the drive home, just as I turned onto our street, I saw a rainbow in the sky. I was so surprised that I stopped and snapped a picture. A beautiful end to a good day. Brought back memories of my early days with Scott, and it felt like a smile from God.

On Sundays after church, I usually visited Scott's grave, which was about ten miles from where we lived. Every road, every stop sign, every store, every section of favorite landscape was filled with memories of Scott. All I had experienced in Goshen had been with him, and now these daily familiar sights served as constant reminders of his absence. Days and miles filled with tears and pain. On this day when I visited,

Scott had been in heaven two months, and I was happy to see that the headstone had been placed on his grave.

I returned to the cemetery, after buying some flowers, and spent a lot of time there praying and taking pictures of the cemetery entrance and the tree-lined drive. Grand old trees formed a canopy over the road, as you entered the cemetery. I did not talk to Scott when I visited; rather, I always looked up through the canopy of the giant limbs overhead and talked and cried with God. This particular day was beautiful with a temp in the high 70's and sunny skies. Listening to the leaves rustling in the breeze was soothing. Two chipmunks were scampering around the tree that shaded Scott's grave, as I listened to the birds singing. No one visited the cemetery while I was there, and I lingered alone. As I was looking up around me, I was filled with the realization that Scott's love for me and my love for him came from God and love never dies. I was still here, because God's purpose for my life had not yet been fulfilled. Later that evening as I was downloading the pictures and reviewing my day, I was struck by the similarities of the drive into the cemetery resembling the tree canopied road in the "Oak Arches" print.

The very next day, I received an unexpected package from one of the ladies on Facebook who had contributed to the recent letter. She sent me a wonderful assortment of handmade soaps, candle tarts, room sprays, a jar candle, and some auto sachets. The aromas were delightful and lifted my spirits tremendously. Her kindness and generosity were another huge hug from God.

A special blessing came in the form of a letter, dated 6/3/2011, from the Batesville Casket Company, Living Memorial Program, with a certificate that stated, "A tree has been placed in a national forest to serve as a memorial for your loved one. Yoder-Culp Funeral Home made this thoughtful request on your family's behalf. This program is administered in cooperation with the Forest Service, United States Department of Agriculture, as part of a major reforestation endeavor. The species and location of the tree are determined by the Forest Service, based upon the greatest reforestation need. Recent plantings have taken place in 15 national forests throughout the country. May you and your family find peace in knowing that the tree planted in honor of your loved one will have a lasting impact on earth. The enclosed certificate acknowledges the fulfillment of the Living Memorial." This was quite unexpected and touched my heart deeply. I shared the news of this beautiful hug from God with Scott's family.

Sue had taken me under her wing--offering prayers, a caring heart, a listening ear, and helping hands for so many tasks. The time of encouragement and fellowship with her at the coffee shop was the highlight of my week outside of church. When I met her on July 5, 2011, she gave me an incredible gift. Several weeks prior, she had asked me to copy some of my favorite pictures with Scott onto a flash drive. She had created a book with those pictures and included her own artwork on the pages, using words spoken by Scott or me that I had shared with her in various conversations over the previous weeks. This book was a beautiful record of my love story with Scott and featured a favorite photo of us on the cover. The title of the book, "Give God the Pieces--He will Patch them Together," was taken from a handmade sign that Scott and I had purchased at an Amish market during my first visit to Indiana for our future home. I was deeply moved by this gift of love and kindness from Sue's heart.

After his death, I could not eat more than a few bites at meals for weeks. I had no interest in food or cooking. One night after mentally reviewing my usual list of options, I decided I would cook. Choosing something simple, I put two biscuits in the oven and started preparing the gravy. As I stood at the stove stirring, I was overwhelmed with an onslaught of memories, and I dropped to my knees in sobbing pain. Scott and I had enjoyed so many happy times in the kitchen. We shared our day, we made weekend plans, we cooked together, we did the dishes together, we laughed and flirted sharing hugs and kisses in the kitchen. The loss of him washed over me anew. I sat on the floor lost in those moments now gone forever. Many months passed with countless takeout containers and paper sacks before I put another pan on the stove.

One of the first things we had purchased after my move to Goshen in 2008 was a tall shepherd's hook and a birdfeeder for the back yard, which was empty of ornamentation save for the empty concrete slab patio and a large yard to mow. A shallow band of woods stretched across the back property line. We had placed the birdfeeder in the open, but close enough to the woods that the birds would feel safe. I had watched the activity around the feeder one afternoon in delight. An acrobatic squirrel had contorted himself to stretch his body over to the feeder after climbing the pole and was feasting. Two chipmunks had scampered up the pole to the feeder--one was standing on the roof, while his friend was running around the outer edge scattering seed all over the ground below. A rabbit had ventured out from the tall grass that bordered the woods to nibble as well, while a pair of doves pecked and bobbed around the pole. We had made a point to keep the feeder filled during the bitter cold winter months to help the birds during heavy snowfalls. I recalled the day in January of 2011 when Scott had gone out to the feeder to refill the seed. Visibly shaken when he walked back into the garage, he explained that while he was at the feeder, he had spotted something against the house close to the patio door. Upon closer inspection, he discovered that it was a dead rabbit. Something had completely eaten the rabbit inside out, leaving only the head and the skin. Scott was not normally squeamish, but he said that was the most disturbing thing he had ever seen. Afterwards, he took the shovel and disposed of the remains in the woods. A sad heaviness started growing in my spirit that persisted for many days afterwards. The memory of that incident was now replaying in my mind.

I then recalled an unsettling dream I had one night soon after moving to Goshen. In the dream, I was in our home office and someone was trying to get into the house. They kept circling around the house over and over and would not go away. The persistence produced fear and anger in the dream. This person was yelling through the window in our bedroom office. Though I could not hear the words, I could feel the intense determination to disrupt our home. I woke up at that point in dismay. At that time, I assumed that I was worried something would take away our happiness. Now, as I was remembering the details of these two incidents, I wondered if I had missed a warning.

Chapter Seven

WRONG TURN

One recurring piece of advice I had read in the different books about grief was not to make any life changing decisions during the first year following a major loss, unless absolutely necessary. Unfortunately, the lease where Scott and I lived was up for renewal and realistically, I could not comfortably afford to pay that rent. The property management company reassured me not to feel pressured to move out by the end of the month and kindly offered to let me stay, until I was able to relocate. I could move to another cheaper place in Goshen, or I could move south to be closer to my children.

My son lived in Knoxville and suggested that I move to Tennessee. The idea appealed to me and seemed logical. Everyone agreed it was a good idea for me to be closer to my family. My son located an apartment complex close to him that I could afford. He visited the office for information and viewed a unit. I started communication with one of the agents over the next few weeks for approval.

I would have to downsize substantially before moving. The house was fully furnished, and the basement and garage were full as well. Sue helped me sort and plan the first yard sale. She brought some friends from her small group, who moved the furniture out to the garage, as well as her folding tables to use for display. I placed an ad and prayed for God's blessing. Sue helped both days with the sale. There were only odds and ends left on the tables at the end of the second day, and we loaded a few boxes into my vehicle to be dropped off for donation. I planned a second sale for all the stuff in the garage and more furniture I had pulled out of the house. Sue stepped in to help, as did Scott's mother. Again, God blessed the sale. I then ran a separate ad to sell all of my primitive furniture pieces, as I had reluctantly accepted the realization that this furniture would not fit into my apartment in Tennessee. One couple saw the ad and drove 60 miles, buying the entire lot and loading it onto their truck. Everything was out of the way, except what I was keeping, and I started packing every day after work and on the weekends. The joy of my last move was missing, and now I was packing with purpose. My move date was set for the last weekend of July in 2011. After checking with various companies about moving, I asked Scott's employer if he knew someone I could hire to drive a moving truck. He graciously offered the use of his trailer. He and his son, along with Scott's parents and brothers, would meet at the house to load the trailer. Anything that would not fit onto the trailer would be loaded onto my father-in-law's truck and taken to their home in Bristol, until I could make arrangements to move it. Chris and his oldest son would drive his trailer down to Knoxville over the weekend to unload.

In light of my upcoming move at the end of July, my mother-in-law planned a family gathering on the 11th. Walking into the lake cottage, my attention was immediately drawn to the huge sheet cake on the dining table. A rainbow was "painted" across the iced cake, and a spray of roses cascaded down one side. After dinner the family presented me with a card and a gift. Each family group had written a message in the card, and Scott's parents had both written their own personal notes. I was not prepared for so many words of love and encouragement from his family and could not hold back the tears. I had not felt this much love from them during my marriage to Scott. The box held a sterling silver locket with two diamond hearts on the front and two pictures inside, one of Scott and one of us--a beautiful treasure from Scott's family.

I took a break from packing and moving preparations on Saturday, July 16, to drive to Ann Arbor, Michigan, to visit with my half-brother, Jay, and his family. We had not seen each since our father died fourteen years prior, and I wanted to see him before my anticipated move to Knoxville at the end of the month. I had tried to arrange a visit during the previous year, but Jay was unable to come and now Scott was gone. My older cousin, Charles, who lived outside Columbus, Ohio, was going to drive to Michigan as well with his wife, Maggie, for a mini family reunion. I had only met him once prior when I was a young child, at Jay's sister's funeral in Michigan. We had started communicating by email and phone earlier in the year. He had spent years researching our family history and wanted to share that information. He had also emailed many pictures I had never seen of other family members. I was very excited to see them and hear their stories, to spend some time with my family, though we did not know each other. There was an age gap of about twenty years between my brother and cousin and me, and we had not lived close to one another at any time in the past. I remembered seeing my brother Jay and his wife, Bev, a few times when I was young. They always stopped and visited with Aunt Lucy when they passed through Memphis.

It was a beautiful day and a pleasant drive, a refreshing change from the familiar routes. I brought along the book Sue had created to show them pictures of Scott. We spent the entire day outside talking about our childhoods and past years, while enjoying a wonderful lunch that Bev had prepared. Jay and Charles both remembered my grandfather, who had died before I was born, and they shared their memories about him and other family members I had not known. I loved the time I spent with them, recognizing the need for that time of connection. We hugged and took pictures of each other and promised to stay in touch. As I drove home late that afternoon, I reflected on the part of our conversation that had centered on Scott's death and faith. I had shared that Scott was saved a few years prior to his death and my peace came from knowing that he was in heaven. Jay shared that he had also been saved and was concerned about some of his children and grandchildren. From what Charles said during that conversation, I gathered that he did not know God. I shared my testimony and told him that I wanted him to spend eternity with me in heaven. He was heavy on my heart as I left Michigan, and I drove many miles praying for him and the other unsaved family members during the return trip to Goshen, as well as thanking God for this time with my family.

Journal entry dated 7/17/2011:

I met the nicest young lady at church today, named Monica, who was sitting at the end of the same row. We exchanged smiles when she took her seat, just as the music started. After the service ended, as I was getting my keys out of my purse, she came over and offered her hand, introducing herself. She shared how long she had been attending Grace Community Church, and I told her how Scott had brought me to his church. She was very interested in my story, so I shared my meeting with Scott, the subsequent move to Goshen, and our marriage. I explained how God had blessed us both in this marriage and that I now feel closer to Him than ever in spite of Scott's move to heaven. We spoke of many things and talked so long that the volunteers had stacked all the chairs and had started mopping the floor (our sanctuary is a gymnasium that serves the community during the week). We continued our conversation during the walk to the parking lot. Monica hugged me and thanked me for ministering to her. She asked if we could get together before I moved, and we exchanged phone numbers. I do not know what I said that lifted Monica, but it made me feel good when she said I had helped her today. I do not understand what happened, but I know it was a good thing, and I look forward to seeing this young woman again before I leave here.

Monica and I subsequently met at "The Chief," a local popular ice cream stand. I felt moved to bring the book that Sue had created and to share more details about my journey in Goshen. She was obviously moved, and I felt a spiritual connection with this young woman.

Journal entry dated July 24, 2011:

"Today felt like multiple mini days. My morning was spent once again sorting, packing, and remembering. I sat down for a break after a few hours and started reading through old emails that Scott and I had exchanged back in 2007-2008. We had exchanged words of love, flirting, and plans. Revisiting those memories triggered tears as well as smiles. How I miss our banter. One email in particular epitomized the difference in our perspectives. Where I tended to look for layers and hidden meanings, Scott would look at the same issue with logic and reason. I had written him with the details of my dream the previous night, about spider webs and one huge spider that I had spent most of the dream trying to get out of my purse. I did not dream very often and hours after I woke up I could still see it vividly in my mind, so I asked Scott for his interpretation. I laughed out loud as I read his response, "I think your dream may be an indication that you feel fear and disdain for spiders." I could almost hear his voice reading those words.

Later in the afternoon, Sue came over to help with some chores. She went with me to the hospital where Scott had been pronounced dead to attend a memorial service for the families and friends of patients who had died at the hospital from January 1st through June 30th. Scott's parents were there, and we all cried together. The service was painful. My mind was spinning around the past memories and the loss of Scott, my upcoming move and last minute to-do details, and the unknown future without Scott. The chaplain read a poem, "Miss Me But Let Me Go," the 23rd Psalm, and Psalm 46, which I will revisit later tonight. We sang "Amazing Grace," which always makes me cry. The service closed with all of us in attendance reading out loud, "The Lord bless us and keep us. The Lord make His face shine on us and be gracious to us. The Lord look upon us with favor and give us peace."

I'm torn between my grief and the necessity to move forward. Part of me wants to stay as is, in a distorted connection to Scott, and the other part is urging me not to sink into a grief rut, because I still have life to live and I cannot thrive in the past. I am dreading the moment I leave our driveway for the last time. I keep reminding myself that Scott has moved to heaven and I am not leaving him in Goshen. It is only through God's love and strength that I am able to start this transition. I look around me--the walls are empty, the furniture is bare, boxes are stacked in the garage and the living room, and I only have a few days left in Indiana. Tomorrow will be another day full of mini days."

I arrived in Knoxville Friday evening on the 29th of July. After checking into the hotel, I met my son for dinner, and we reviewed our plan for the next day. I made it an early night, anticipating a good night's rest; however, I did not sleep well. I had a sense of unrest in my soul. I had prayed and talked to the Lord about this move, and until this moment had thought I was doing the right thing, but something was not quite right. My son and I met at the apartment complex the next morning. We reviewed the lease and then drove around to the building where I would be living. There were many buildings, and I was on the very end at the back of the complex. I had trusted my son's judgment that this was a nice place and had tried to keep a positive attitude about this move and leaving Goshen only four months after Scott's death.

My heart fell as we entered the apartment. The place was filthy. Everything was dirty. It appeared the previous tenant had just vacated the property and nothing had been cleaned. A ceiling fan was on high speed situated over the dining area, but the ceiling was too low for the fan, and I was afraid to walk in that area. We looked in all the rooms. The carpets were disgusting, and my spirits sank lower as we moved through each room. The kitchen was nasty and the fridge was old and dirty. When the agent tried to open the pantry door, it struck the light fixture, which was hanging from the ceiling.

At this point, my son looked at me and said, "Mom, you cannot live here." He was voicing my own thoughts, and I spoke in agreement. The leasing agent was irritated and assured me there were no other units available. I thanked her for her time, and we left the apartment with no idea of what to do next.

My son and I simultaneously let out a huge sigh once we were away from the agent. He suggested we go to a coffee shop and use his laptop to search for another place. I called Scott's employer and my in-laws to update them on the situation. I had been so sure of this place that I had already forwarded my mail to this address. Details and arrangements were jostling around in my head as we sat down. We pulled up property management company listings, and then the realization struck me that I had no proof of employment, as I was self-employed and had nothing with me to show income. All of my papers were in a file cabinet on the trailer back in Indiana.

My son suggested searching for listings of rental property by an individual. We called about the properties that included a phone number and emailed a message to the other listings. Hopeful that someone would respond, we went to dinner and planned to check back later for responses. To my dismay, no one had responded to any of our phone messages or emails. With sinking spirits, we contacted the listings again. We visited awhile in the hotel and tried to be optimistic about the next day. I called Scott's parents and employer to let them know I had no place to live as of yet. I went up to my room, and as the time slowly passed, I was filled with a quiet, but firm assurance that I needed to go back to Goshen. This move was not God's plan. He had been with me every moment since Scott moved to heaven, and I could physically feel His absence. I had not asked Him prior to this decision and had decided to make this move based on my own thoughts and the approval of others. As I read my Bible that night and prayed and talked to God, I knew I was going back to Indiana. The next morning, I met my son for breakfast. Again, there had been no response to our emails or phone messages. I told him I was returning to Goshen. We hugged and said goodbye, and with tears in my eyes and heaviness in my heart, I started the journey north.

Chapter Eight

RETURN TO GOSHEN

I drove back to Indiana wondering what to do and praying for guidance. My in-laws offered their house in Bristol temporarily, as they spent the summers at their lake cottage in Michigan. I was exhausted physically and emotionally by the time I arrived in Indiana and very thankful to have a bed and shower.

I needed the Internet for my work and was very distressed when I discovered that the service provider at their house could not support my work apps. I was scheduled to be back online for work the next day. Scott's employer offered to let me work in an unused office space at his company temporarily. All of my belongings, including my clothing in wardrobe boxes, was still packed on his trailer, with the remainder stored in my in-laws' garage and dining room. I offered to rent a storage unit so he would have the use of his trailer, but he assured me that he would not need it until Fall, and he would prefer to leave it loaded until I was settled into my own place. Inwardly, I sighed in relief that I would not have to deal with it at the moment on top of everything else. My car looked like I was living out of it, as I still had many odd things that would not pack in a box riding around with me on a daily basis. I had only packed a few changes of clothes, jeans and t-shirts, and I washed all my clothes in one load every five days. I had what I needed to live--food, shelter, clothing, and a place to work. Most important, I had peace in my soul that I had made the right decision in returning to Goshen.

Journal entry dated 8/12/2011:

God delivered, once again, today. My paycheck that has been floating around since mid-July finally arrived back in Goshen today! I was so sure of my anticipated move that I had already forwarded my mail effective July 29. This check, which should have been delivered before I left Indiana, was misdelivered somewhere else in town, forwarded to TN, returned, and then forwarded to my new address. Thank you Lord! To celebrate, I got a sandwich to go from Subway and went to a local park to eat lunch. It's a glorious day here--about 80, blue sky, no humidity, and nice breeze. I took a walk afterwards just soaking up this good day!

Ironically, although I was staying at Scott's childhood home and using space at the office where he had worked, I did not feel sad in those environments. Maybe it was because we had not shared any memories in those places. Though awkward to return to Goshen and admit I was wrong, I believed it would be worse to waste years traveling the wrong path, as I had done in the past. I needed to be still and to be quiet...to just be, and hopefully discover God's purpose for me without Scott. My return to Goshen was not understood, and at times, I sensed resentment and aggravation from those who were burdened by my presence once again. I remembered unkind words that had been voiced following the death of Scott, but I also recalled the constant tender presence of the Holy Spirit. I wanted God's approval more than the acceptance of the people my life was impacting at that time, and I chose to focus on Him.

Sometimes, people land in our lives, and we do not understand why or what we are supposed to do with them. We may have asked God to use us to be of service to Him, to let us be a blessing to others, but when

He brings a need we balk because it is not what we envisioned. This person is not who we want to help. We want to help someone who will make us feel good about ourselves, someone we are familiar with, someone who will bring us recognition, someone we have determined who deserves our help. We feel indignant when pushed beyond our limit and seek affirmation from others about our generosity once a person becomes a burden. God brings a need, a test, and gives us the freedom to respond. The trial is never just about the person affected, and there is a much bigger picture developing that cannot be seen at that time. The realization that I was the person who had been thrust into the midst of these strangers' lives, with the uncomfortable awareness of their struggle to step up or turn away, was totally humbling. I had lived independently for many years prior to Scott and had been able to manage by myself or hire help when I needed it; however, upon Scott's death, I did not know who to ask for help, and I turned to the people he had trusted. I needed the help of these people and could offer nothing in return, except a thank-you with a silent prayer for God's blessings on their service. Showing the love of Jesus to others who are not of our choosing, especially when other family members do not share the same conviction, is very difficult. I asked God to bless those servant hearts in a special way.

My life was simple, consisting of work, reading, prayer and conversation with God, and church on Sunday. The solitude was not entirely painful. I was in a period of amazing spiritual growth and revelation during this time of grieving and healing. I walked in two different realities, reacting and responding to current events and people around me, while holding onto Scott in our shared past. The Holy Spirit had awakened an awareness of His presence, and I was completely in awe of His grace and mercy. God began to reveal things about my past, my relationship with Scott, and about Him. My spiritual life grew tremendously, while my physical life was very dormant, and I walked in peace and joy in the midst of these unsettled circumstances. Though my future was uncertain and my daily life was following an unfamiliar pattern, I had assurance in my spirit that everything was going to be okay. I had no one to talk to, so I shared everything with the Lord, every moment of pain, hurt, loss, and emptiness. The more of my pain and sorrow that I gave to God, the more of Him I received in return. Through tears, I shared my thoughts and feelings and memories with God in detail, and He filled me with more of His love and presence in exchange. I needed His strength to carry me through every dreary day.

I missed Scott every second of every minute. I longed to hear his voice again, to hold him, to see his charming smile, and I spent more than one weekend reviewing our email messages. Reading his words again reminded me of what we had and what was now gone. I laughed and smiled at many of the messages, but one in particular grabbed my heart, dated October 2, 2007.

"Good morning Baby.

Something has been weighing heavy on my mind and I feel now is the time to say something... I believe God woke me at 4 a.m. and said, 'NOW!'...lol I can see you rolling your eyes as you start to read this, but keep in mind, I'm sincere and honest about this and it's not the details, but the subject that's very important to me.

There is another element to your communication with 'Michael' (a blogger) that bothers me and I realize now what it is... something that you and I are missing... the open discussion about God. I see your kind offerings of prayers and blessings to him, like just yesterday, 'Hope you feel the blessing of God's love today'... I would be hard pressed to find a comment of that nature in my comments or in our conversation. You share something vitally important with him that you and I don't share. It's not so much a feeling of jealousy of him; it's more a feeling of distance from you. That's not entirely honest... there is a twinge of jealousy there because I feel 'Michael' is getting a part of you that I don't get, (not the well-wishes, but the spiritual side of you and the open discussion of God.)... but it really has little to do with him personally. I'm sure if I were to write a blog on any subject including God, you would comment on it. The thing is, you and I are closer than blogs, but still don't communicate in that fashion. I sense that you don't regard me as being on your level when it comes to spiritual matters, and maybe I'm not, but I don't think you should hold back your thoughts and feelings, waiting for me to catch up with you spiritually.

Another instance that got my attention ...and I'd like you to think about it, bearing in mind that I realize this may be meaningless in your mind, but at the time it seemed to me a clear indication. Awhile back you left a message for many of your outwardly Christian friends, some-thing to the effect of, 'face it, God loves you'... I thought that was a wonderful message... I also couldn't help but notice I wasn't included. It struck me then... you may not think of me in that light.

I don't blame YOU for this Sweetheart, I realize I'm not as open and vocal about God as I should be and that's something I need to work on and pray about. I've always been a very private person about most personal matters and my faith has often been included in that privacy. You are strong in your faith and very open and vocal about it. I just ask that you don't push me away or distance yourself in that area because you may not perceive me to be as outwardly expressive about God. I truly believe it takes three for a successful marriage and I think we need to be more inclusive of God if we're going to have His blessing.

I love you with all my heart, Iris. I hope this isn't too heavy so early in the morning and I'd like to know your thoughts on this. (No rush).

P.S. Please don't go overboard regarding 'Michael'. I'm not asking or suggesting that you stop the comments to him. I trust your love for me and I certainly don't want to do anything to squelch your growth spiritually. He has many good things on his page… my intention is not to keep you from that, but to share more of those ideas with you.

Have a wonderful day Sweetheart."

Conviction had overwhelmed me when I initially read his painfully honest words in 2007. I had been unaware that I was not giving Scott the same spiritual encouragement and attention as I shared with virtual strangers on that social media page, and the hurt in his heart pierced through my spiritual blindness. I remembered that after his message, we had talked extensively about our spiritual convictions and beliefs, and I apologized sincerely for slighting him. I had been praying for him on a regular basis, but he could not hear those prayers. He wanted and needed to physically hear praise and encouragement on a spiritual basis from me to him specifically.

As I re-read his message from 2007, I confessed any failure on my part to honor God or Scott during our relationship and marriage. I had never regarded myself as more spiritual than Scott, or anyone else for that matter, and indeed had believed that he was the better person in our relationship. I was very surprised that he perceived me as the stronger partner spiritually. He had not known that though I encouraged and prayed for others, I had never believed that God loved me just as much as the people I lifted in prayer. I had not accepted God's love for me, until after Scott moved to heaven. Tears flowed with those memories and revelation. I asked God once again to bless Scott's soul.

Scott's sudden and unexpected death was a shock to all who knew him, and everyone wanted to understand why he had been taken home so soon. Some assumed that my past sin, or Scott's past sin, or perhaps some continued sin had led to judgment. Rather than asking, "Why," my question was, "God, what are you doing?" He had orchestrated our meeting, blessed our marriage with beautiful healing love, and then had taken Scott home quietly in the early morning hours. What was next? I was grieving, while striving to face forward. I believe God kept me in Goshen, so He could have my undivided attention for healing, revelation and growth, and to prepare me for the next step, whatever that may be and wherever it may lead. I chose to be grateful for those precious years with Scott, because without God, I would never have known that love and happiness.

Death brings revelations that would not be revealed otherwise. After moving to Goshen, whenever I was asked how Scott and I had met, I would give the same simple honest answer--that God had brought us together and blessed us with an amazing love and marriage. Following his death, I realized that people had not accepted the truth. Uglier motives were suggested, that our relationship was based solely on physical attraction and sex; that perhaps Scott thought I had money; that I thought Scott had money or would receive an inheritance upon his parents' death. I was reminded of God's Word that says the mouth speaks what is in the heart, and I viewed everyone around me differently. I was grieving and hurting, yet I had to make allowances for these misguided remarks and questions. Perhaps the love Scott and I shared was more rare and special than even I had realized.

The enemy, ever ready with an explanation, dumped condemnation on me for my past mistakes and behavior. He repeatedly tried to convince me of the lie that God had punished me for my sin by taking Scott. I prayed and began to confess every sin I could remember, even if I had confessed it previously. I asked God to reveal any unconfessed sin remaining in my heart. Prayer and understanding of my identity in Christ stopped the condemnation and lies that had been playing in my head. Through time in the Word and prayer, I accepted Scott's death as part of God's plan. I read the scriptures about death, returning to Psalm 139:16 more than once, "Your eyes saw my unformed body; all the days ordained for me were written in your book before one of them came to be." (NIV) God knew how many years Scott would live before he was born, and He knew how many years Scott and I would have together when we met.

I had peace that God was in control and Scott was with Him after reaching the end of his journey on earth. I did not know all the details and many questions would remain unanswered this side of eternity, but I knew I could trust God completely without any reservations. He had reassured me to accept and receive the love from Scott, to leave everything familiar behind and move to Goshen, and He had blessed me abundantly while my life was undergoing complete change. I reflected on how dreary life would have continued had I not trusted His guidance. I would not have experienced the amazing love we shared or this wonderful relationship with God. Somehow, as only God can, He was healing my heart from all the hurt and rejection of the past, as I continued through my grief journey.

I had lived five decades without really knowing God, carrying the lies from childhood into adulthood. The wrong impression of God and of myself had affected all of my life decisions and choices. God, in His mercy, had not abandoned me despite my rejection of Him. Instead of punishing me for my sexual sin on that dark night in the hotel, He brought love into my life that far exceeded my dreams--sweet, powerful, healing, amazing love. During this special season with God, He replayed past events and showed me that He had been pursuing me throughout my life. The realization that I had sabotaged my own happiness and blessings multiple times in the past was hard to accept, and I felt the weight of all those wasted years and energy and resources. What-if scenarios ran through my mind, but God was gracious and merciful. I needed to see the truth in order to better understand myself and God. All of the pain and defeat in my life were from the enemy, and I had resigned myself to loss and lack, because I had not known or trusted God.

In March of 2011, Japan suffered a high magnitude earthquake followed by a devastating tsunami. I attended church as usual on the first Sunday in April. The worship music was inspiring, and Pastor Brown delivered a powerful message. Then something very special happened. He invited the congregation to take off their shoes and bring them up front, stacking them across the stage. All of the shoes would be donated to the survivors in Japan, most of whom had lost everything. He said he knew we were probably wearing our favorite shoes and he was asking us to make a small sacrifice to help those in great need. I felt a punch in my abdomen and I winced in pain, as I looked down at the silver and burgundy Asics shoes I was wearing. Scott had taken me to an athletic store in Mishawaka and waited patiently inside, while the store assistant observed my gait in the parking lot. She had measured my foot and suggested the shoe styles that would fit my needs. I had tried on three different styles, and the Asics had fit the best. These were the most expensive athletic shoes I had ever worn and they were a gift from Scott. Tears welled up, as I untied my shoes and removed them from my feet. I stood up, cradling the shoes in my arms, and followed other members to the front of the church. I prayed as I walked forward down the aisle that God would deliver these shoes to someone who needed to feel His love in a profound way, just as I had received tremendous love from my husband through his many gifts. When I returned to my seat, a woman sitting a few seats over asked me what we were going to do now. Smiling through my tears, I answered that we were going to leave the church in our sock feet.

The funeral home had sent a letter offering grief counseling soon after Scott's burial. I was not interested at that time, but after several weeks of grieving alone, I called to enroll. Unfortunately, the sessions were not ongoing and would not be available again until Fall. I had explained that I was planning to move and would not be able to attend. Incredibly, after my move back to Goshen and another address change, I received a forwarded letter from the funeral home in August again offering grief counseling. These sessions were scheduled to start in September and continue through February, meeting once a week, every other week. I was very thankful for this opportunity, and I called to sign up. I did not know what to expect as I was driving to the funeral home for the first session, but I had prayed and believed this would help with my grieving. There was a large group at the first meeting. Most of us welcomed the opportunity to talk about our loved ones and to share our stories, but a few of the women would not talk and did not return.

Although some of the people in the group had family around them, their families had not been very supportive and did not know how to handle their loved ones' grief. I bonded with this group at the first meeting, and a core of six became my grief family. We contacted each other on our painful anniversaries and prayed for one another. We met once a month for social interaction and conversation that provided a measure of comfort and stability in our otherwise unsettled lives. We understood the need to talk about our spouses and share memories of our marriages as a necessary part of healing. We had all experienced attempts by the people around us to change the subject or to cut off the conversation when we talked about our spouses. The counseling sessions and times we spent together provided needed support during our grief that we did not have with family or other friends.

Sometimes, in the midst of numb pain, the smallest details can make an impact on a hurting heart. The funeral home provided a comfortable setting for the grief sessions in a private parlor room that was carpeted with nice couches and chairs. There was a large round table set up for us covered with a fabric tablecloth corresponding to the current season. China plates, silverware, glasses, and coffee cups with saucers were provided for our use. A large clear pitcher of water full of ice cubes always adorned the table, as well as coffee and condiments. One of the women at the funeral home baked a special treat for our every meeting. These were all special touches of love to comfort strangers gathered to share pain and memories.

A pastor and his wife led our meetings with prayer and a devotional followed by discussion about specific situations. In anticipation of the upcoming Christmas holiday, the pastor's wife provided us with clear glass ornaments as a project. We were to gather small mementos of our loved ones and bring those to the next meeting. Each of us would take a turn filling our ornament and share the significance of the items we were placing into the glass ball. I went shopping with one of the women in the group, and we found some small charms and other miniatures that reflected the interests of our spouses. I also searched for pictures on the Internet to print and cut out to use in my ornament.

At our next meeting, I filled my ball with tiny tools, a coffee stamp, white snowflake sequins, large red heart sequins, a scrap of the wrapping paper Scott had used to wrap the "Oak Arches" picture, a small piece of the Christmas letterhead Scott had used for my letter from Santa, a miniature baseball glove and small wooden bat, a gift tag with Scott's handwriting, a bowling pin and ball charm, golf ball stickers, a camera charm, and the small pictures I had cut out and rolled up to fit into the opening. Two charms adorned the ornament cap hanger, one representing our marriage and the other his love of coffee. The ball was stuffed when I finished. I displayed it on an ornament hanger inside my curio cabinet. This ornament represented the life of the most wonderful man I had ever known and would not be packed away when the season ended.

Journal entry, dated September 13, 2011:

I woke up around 4 a.m. and could not go back to sleep. After tossing and turning about 20 minutes, I got out of bed and went into the living room to see if there was anything worth watching on T.V. Usually every channel is hawking some infomercial; however, I found a Christian minister on one channel speaking about marriage. He was explaining what a wife really means when a husband asks her, "What's wrong?" and she answers, "Nothing." He said a guy was talking to his friend and told him that his wife was on her knees before him the previous evening.

His friend said, "WOW! What did she say?" She told him, "Come out from under that bed and fight like a man!" I laughed out loud...something about his delivery and the audience reaction just tickled me!! I realized this was the first time I had laughed at 4 a.m. since Scott died and the laughter felt good. I went back to bed and fell asleep. I love these small enlightening moments.

I visited Scott's favorite steakhouse in celebration of what would have been our three-year anniversary in October of 2011. The empty seat across from me in the booth served as another reminder that he was gone. My daily life was filled with painful reminders, and some days moved liked a revolving door of pain and tears. The tears, at times, flowed without warning. Grief triggers, as we learned in counseling, could occur any time. I was aware every moment of every day of my husband's absence. Fighting back the tears, I took a deep breath and determined I would observe this day in his honor. When we celebrated special occasions with a nice dinner, he always chose steak, while my preference was seafood. Today, I ordered a steak and enjoyed my meal in relative peace, as I refocused my thoughts to happier times.

I glanced around at other people in the restaurant, while I ate, and my eyes rested on a middle-aged couple who appeared to be completely disconnected. They did not talk and even avoided looking at one another. I kept my gaze moving so as not to stare, but my eyes drifted back to that table several times during my meal. Sadness filled me, as I watched them eat in total silence. Would it make a difference in their behavior if one of them woke in the morning to find their partner had moved into eternity? Would they have something to say in these last few hours--an offering of forgiveness, a profession of love, anything that would be a comfort the next day? Scott and I had exchanged our "I love you's" and goodnight kisses as usual on his final day on earth, but I would have said so much more had I known it was our last night together. I lifted a prayer of gratitude for the love we shared and for our complete enjoyment of each other. I also prayed for the disconnected couple. I was not angry at God when Scott died; instead, I was thankful for the love, as I had failed miserably in my efforts to find the love that God had given me unconditionally. Upon Scott's death, I had feared that our love had died, but in a wondrous way that I did not understand, the love was still present and was growing stronger.

A few weeks later, I moved into a duplex in Goshen. The same people who had helped me previously rallied together once again to unload the trailer and move the furniture into my new home. The washer and dryer were connected in the basement, and I had plenty of storage. I had always found basements to be a little creepy, but this was a modern build. The walls and floor were concrete and dry, with four light fixtures and the required egress window providing natural light as well. All the boxes I did not immediately need were stacked in the basement to unpack at my leisure. We retrieved all the belongings that were stored in my in-laws' garage and dining room, as well and brought those back to my place. I was very grateful for this extra help and asked God to bless those kind hands and hearts abundantly once again.

The next evening, I heard a sound coming from the basement like an alarm blaring, and the tone reminded me of the alarm clock that had sounded just hours after Scott's move to heaven. That same clock was now on my nightstand, and I could not remember packing away another clock with an alarm. The sound was definitely louder when I opened the basement door, and I walked down the steps somewhat hesitantly. I could not tell which box the noise was coming from as I walked around the rows of boxes, and I went back upstairs. The alarm sounded all day and the next night. I had hoped the battery would weaken and the alarm would shut off, but it persisted without fading. I made up mind the following day to find the source. Determined, I went downstairs with a utility knife to open boxes in my search. I discovered the noise was coming from a very large box of candy dispensers that I had collected and received as gifts over the years while working in the office, prior to moving to Goshen. Periodically, I changed the dispenser on my desk to share candy with my coworkers, and other employees would donate money or candy to help keep the dispenser filled. I opened the large box in front of me and started removing the contents. The alarm was irritatingly loud, sounding from one particular dispenser with a clock. I had put a battery in the clock during the time I used it at work, but I had never set the alarm on the clock and it had never sounded during the previous years. Now, somehow, the alarm had been triggered. I felt a sense of triumph as I shut it off.

I decided to carry a couple of boxes upstairs with me to unpack and to start a load of laundry. I set the hamper down at the basement door, turned on the lights, and then started down the basement steps. As I was loading the washer, the overhead lights started waxing and waning. There were four separate plain light bulb fixtures mounted on the ceiling, and all four bulbs were brightening and dimming simultaneously. This happened three times, and then the lights all went out at the same time. I stood there calmly, fighting back fear, and this scripture came to mind, "Greater is He who is in me than He who is in the world." I spoke those words out loud, as I walked across the floor to the light switch and turned the lights back on, finished loading the washer, and went back upstairs. The first box I opened contained pictures and the bowling trophy I had given Scott as a gag gift. I had purchased an old bowling pin at a flea market and ordered an engraved metal plate to read, "Strike King," with two small holes drilled at the top of the plate. I had draped the plate around the neck of the pin with a chain. He kept the trophy on his desk at home, and I smiled at the memory of our bowling nights, as I set it on the floor by the hutch in the living room.

I finished displaying the pictures and then returned to the basement to transfer the laundry into the dryer. While I was downstairs, the lights began waxing and waning and then went off again. As I was walking towards the light switch, I heard a thud upstairs. The lights would not come on even though I flipped the switch several times. There were two switches--one at the top of the steps and one at the bottom. Fear was starting to build, and I quoted the same scripture out loud, as I walked up the stairs. The switch at the top of the steps would not turn on the lights either, and anxiety was growing over the source of that thud. When I walked back into the living room, the bowling pin had been knocked over and was lying on its side. Completely unnerved at this point, I remembered the prayer I received following Scott's death to pray in our house. I located those papers and started praying in every room of the duplex including the closets, garage, and basement. Later that day, I dropped off a contribution at our church for an upcoming event and asked if one of the pastors would be able to speak to me for a few minutes. Pastor Jeremiah, who had officiated Scott's funeral, met me at the front desk. I shared with him the events in the basement and the bowling pin. He kindly counseled me about spiritual warfare and prayed over me as well. I thanked him for his time and felt reassured and confident as I drove home. There were no further incidents while I lived in that duplex.

Journal entry dated 11/18/2011:

"Just made a quick run to the grocery store. I was delighted to see new coffee mugs and the Christmas decorations on display at the Starbucks kiosk! This year they are offering a four-pack of ornaments. Scott loved Starbucks and took pride in teaching me to appreciate 'real coffee'! Our first year together we started our Starbucks Christmas tree, decorated with just Starbucks ornaments. I had found some of the older coffee stickers used previously to label the bags of coffee and made simple ornaments with cardstock. We subsequently added the store ornaments. Memories rushed in like a flood. As I stood there mentally reminiscing, I noticed a couple approaching the kiosk. The woman was ooohing and ahhhing over the ornaments and the man with her was waiting patiently-- a mirror image of Scott and me. I could feel the prick of tears, but it did not hurt; God put his arm around me and all I felt was the love. I bought the ornaments and a bag of Christmas blend. I will put up my Starbucks tree either this weekend or over Thanksgiving. I am brewing a pot of coffee now and it smells delicious. The years with Scott were few, but the memories are so beautiful and the love has grown stronger in his absence. Thank you, Lord."

I had continued to exchange emails and phone calls with my cousin, Charles, after our meeting in Michigan earlier in the year. He called and invited me to spend Thanksgiving with him and Maggie and their sons and grandchildren in Ohio, which would be about a four-hour drive. Though I wanted to see them, there was a part of me that did not want to be around anyone during the holiday. Scott had only been gone eight months and the tears were continuing to flow, and I did not want to put a damper on other people's enjoyment. Charles assured me they wanted to see me and finally persuaded me to commit. I felt a little lift in my spirit once I made the decision to spend Thanksgiving with them. Later that week, I received a note from Charles in the mail along with some money for the gas expense. I was touched by his thoughtfulness and genuine desire for my company.

The drive to Ohio was uneventful and pleasant, a bright day of sunshine and dry weather. Charles and Maggie welcomed me warmly, and I immediately felt at ease in their home. We talked for hours, before and after Thanksgiving dinner. I met their sons and their wives and children, and pets as well, and we all participated in the conversation. Later in the evening, after I had retired to my bedroom for the night, I marveled at the unexpected enjoyment of the day and the blessing of the time we had spent together. Grieving had been replaced by love and laughter for this rejuvenating short reprieve, strengthening me to endure the pain that would return.

Shortly before my move to Goshen, I had chipped a tooth. There was no associated pain and in the excitement of my new life, I had forgotten about the tooth. Soon after Thanksgiving, I began experiencing pain occasionally in that broken tooth. I dreaded a visit to the dentist, because I knew there were more issues than just this tooth. My retainers had broken brackets, which I had been wearing since my 20's, and I was more than two years late on my checkup. I prayed about the expense, as I had lost my insurance upon Scott's death.

I worked at home and listened to worship music on the local Christian radio station, WFRN, every day. Around the time the pain started in my tooth, a radio promotion began for the "Aegis Dental Group 12 Days of Christmas $15,000 Smile Giveaway". This group was giving away $1,000 of dental care per day until December 12th when the grand prize of $3,000 would be awarded. I heard the promotion several times, as it aired often throughout the day. Several days before the giveaway started, as I was listening to the promotion play again, I heard a voice say, "You'll win." Startled, I remained seated in my chair, unmoving, questioning if I had actually heard the words or if it was just wishful thinking. I heard the words again, "You'll win." It was not an audible voice in the room; rather, it was more like I heard it in my upper chest. I printed an entry form, according to the promotion instructions, and mailed it to the dental group.

I listened every day for the daily winner's name to be announced, while a seesaw of disbelief and reassurance rocked back and forth in my head. On the fifth day of the giveaway, Tuesday, December 6, 2011, my name was announced as the daily winner. I jumped up out of my chair and screamed in delighted surprise! I listened to hear my name again, just to be sure, as the winners' names were announced more than once during the day. I received a confirmation email with instructions to print the attached certificate and to bring it with me to my appointment. I thanked the Lord for His provision, in awe of His love.

Nervous excitement mixed with a little apprehension filled me as I walked into the dental group on December 13th at 9:30 a.m. Impressions were made and x-rays taken along with an exam of my teeth. A treatment plan was written with all costs listed separately and a grand total at the bottom. The dentist explained all the problems in my mouth. The expenses totaled about $300 over the $1000 prize. While he was talking, I was mentally calculating how much I could pay and wondering if I could make payments on the balance. He was called out of the room for a moment, and when he returned, to my great surprise, he said, "I do not know what all you have been through, but I am going to let this certificate cover all the costs involved with your dental care." Gratitude and tears rushed out of me at the same time. I knew instantly, without any doubt, that God had moved in this man's heart. He had provided completely for my need. Many months later, I heard Joseph Prince speak about Bible numerology and learned that five is the number for Grace. I was the winner on the fifth day. Grace abounding.

In an effort to keep from focusing solely on my losses during the holiday season, I looked for opportunities to encourage or help others. A local church was designated as a collection center for Operation Christmas Child and the drop-off date was mid-November. I spent one weekend shopping and filling several boxes, praying over each one for the children who would receive them. My heart lifted, as I imagined the smiles of the children thousands of miles away as they opened their boxes in delight. I stuffed each one as full as possible and dropped them off the next week. I also donated groceries to a local food bank and supported a few charities. Giving helped ease the pain and lifted my spirits.

I spent most of the holiday season in solitude and reflection. My children were able to spend a few days with me, which lifted my heart tremendously, but after they left, I wanted the holidays to pass. I listened to Christmas music, which I love, and cried and prayed through the days and nights. I was married at age 49 and widowed at 52. Love had come late and left too soon. I relived our first meeting and the concerns in my mind at that time. The only real fear I had about Scott was our age difference. I had dated men older than me or close to my age, but not younger. My search during the Internet dating specified an age range of 50-55. I was mortified when Scott shared his age of 39 when we started talking in 2006. I was 47 at that time and my thoughts immediately jumped to my appearance and to the future. Studying myself in the mirror, I had wondered if I appeared almost ten years older than Scott.

What if I did not age well? Would I be mistaken for his older sister or, worse, his mother? What if one day he woke up and did not recognize the old woman lying next to him? Fear and insecurity escalated, while I was fighting to think rationally. Scott reassured me that my age was not a factor, and after we met, the numbers were of no consequence. There were surprised reactions from others when I began to share details about Scott with friends and coworkers. My children teased me a little, but after meeting him, they were of the same opinion that there did not seem to be any age difference. I had prayed that God would bless Scott to always see me as beautiful as he did when we met and that he would never lose his desire for me. I had focused on something that was not even an issue. We only had a short time and nothing had faded. God had known the best man for me, defying all of the search parameters I had used in my own efforts, and if I had just waited on Him after the dream in 2005, I would have spared myself the shame and guilt I experienced before meeting Scott.

Journal entry dated 1/9/2012:

"I had a realization today. God is placing me in the paths of people according to His purpose. This was revealed today as I was reflecting on the grief counseling leaders and other people in my grief family. I continue to praise God through my pain when speaking during our meetings. Now I understand that God wants my testimony heard so others can "hear" or "see" the Holy Spirit through my story. He puts me around others who are not like me for this reason. Instead of focusing on the differences and questioning why I always feel out of place, God wants me to be His witness for those whose faith is weak or who do not know God. This revelation gives me an entirely different perspective. I have asked Him to use me as a vessel and He has been trying to all along. How patient God is with His sheep! My personal motto for 2012 is, 'MY LIMITS ARE UNKNOWN' !!!"

One Saturday afternoon I was lounging in the living room, browsing the Internet on my computer. Outside the sky was gray and the snow was blowing in a frenzy from the high winds. I shivered slightly in response, thankful to be warm and safe inside. As I was viewing this cold day through the patio doors, a pair of bluebirds suddenly landed on the steps outside, facing me through the glass. They remained motionless for about twenty seconds, while tiny snowflakes collected on their feathers. Peace and joy surged through my heart, and I knew this was a touch from God of His love and presence.

On January 25, 2012, I made a note in my journal:

"Sometimes when we pray for someone, God uses us as part of that help, working through us. Scary thought, but when He calls us we cannot be defeated. I'm encouraged by the spiritual growth and blessings that will be revealed through the walk."

Valentine's Day was especially painful in 2012. The tears started flowing soon after I woke up, and I had to push myself to start working, unprepared for the deep hurt that had started early in the day. Scott and I had celebrated this day five times together, and the loss today was much sharper than in the past lonely years prior to meeting Scott. We would never make special memories together again. Mid-morning, there was a knock at the door. A florist delivered a glorious vase of red and pink roses, lilies, and daisies. Surprised, I opened the small envelope and smiled, as I read the loving message on the flower card from my precious daughter. This beautiful arrangement lifted my spirits and reminded me that I am not alone and I am loved.

Our last formal grief meeting was on February 16th. This group had been a source of friendship and encouragement over the past six months. I felt another kind of grief with the end of these meetings, and several of us shared the same emotions. We were not ready to let go of each other and decided to keep meeting on a personal level once a month either at a restaurant or at someone's home. We appointed Beverley as our group leader and called ourselves "Petunia's Pals" at her suggestion! Those were special times of fellowship, and I thanked God for these connections and prayed for each person in the group on a regular basis.

On February 22, 2012, eleven months to the day of Scott's departure, I received an email from the church office informing me that his high school class ring had been found recently in a box that someone had bought at a garage sale. The people who bought the box were holding onto it and wondered how to reach me to see if I would like to have the ring. The letter gave the names of the couple and their phone number and asked if I would call them in response. As I read the message, joy and tears surged through my entire body and heart. I could hardly breathe as I reread the message. Scott had told me about his class ring after I moved here. While I was unpacking my personal things, I had showed him my high school class ring. He shared that his ring had been missing for several years before we met. He had kept it in a box in a dresser drawer when he discovered that it was missing and believed that someone who had been visiting in his home had taken the ring.

The man who answered the phone informed me that the ring was in a small blue mechanic's chest type box with multiple drawers…the type you would keep in a garage to store loose screws, nuts and bolts, etc. He and his wife had bought the box at a yard sale several months prior and had placed it in their garage. Recently, he had gone out to his garage and was looking in the drawers. He pulled out one drawer that held plastic anchors and the ring was resting in the midst of these. I felt a strong thud in my chest....could it be??? I had sold two metal boxes like this at a yard sale last summer in preparation for my move to Knoxville, one blue and one gray that I had brought with me when I moved to Goshen. I remembered an older couple had bought both boxes at my second yard sale. I knew in my spirit that God had returned this ring, and I smiled, as I caught the connection with the drawer of anchors. I had used multiple anchors in my apartment where I lived when I met Scott, for shelving and heavy pictures and other decor, and God had placed the ring in a pile of those same anchors. Realization also dawned that God had become my life anchor.

I met the wife the next day at their house, which was only a few blocks from where I lived, and asked how she had located me. She explained that the ring was a nice ring and looked out of place in that chest of assorted hardware. Scott's signature was engraved inside the ring band, instead of the traditional initials, and the idea occurred to her to check obituaries online. She found his name in her search and the information included the name of our church. They did not attend Grace Community Church, but knew several people who did. The first person she asked did not know Scott's name. Later at a ballgame she asked another friend, who was familiar with his name, and this was the lady who sent me the email message.

I prayed over the wife, thanking God for placing the ring in the hands of trustworthy people, and asked Him to bless her and her husband for their kindness and generosity and efforts to return the ring. I gave her a hug, smiling through tears, thanking her multiple times. My heart was overflowing. The ring did not fit my finger, and I placed it on a chain around my neck. I had received a miracle from God with the return of this long lost ring that was so special to Scott. Reassurance and gratitude flooded through me that Scott was with God, that God was with me, and that all was well. I have continued to wear the ring every day as a reminder of God's faithfulness and love.

I called his parents to share the news and left a voicemail. His mother responded through an email message that she was overwhelmed and would call me later. I joined their next family gathering to share the details and to show the ring to his parents and brothers. We were all amazed at this unexpected blessing.

God blessed Scott's family in a very special way one month later, on the one year anniversary of his move to heaven. One of his nieces and her husband were expecting their second child in early March. During a recent family gathering, while the conversation was focused on the upcoming anniversary of Scott's death, she had made the comment that she did not remember the exact date. The remainder of the subsequent conversation had centered on her due date and excitement over this new addition to the family. Her projected due date came and went, and the days continued to pass. Around 5 a.m. on the 22nd of March, 2012, the baby was born. God had brought life one year later on the same day that Scott had moved to heaven. From now on, the family would have a reason to rejoice on that day in spite of their loss. I was deeply moved by God's mercy and compassion on Scott's family.

In past years, I had wanted to sponsor a child through a Christian organization, but had never followed through in the sponsorship. I had never shared that desire with anyone. In early 2012, WFRN hosted a radiothon for Compassion International, and I was prompted in my spirit to call. I visited the website, finding many children in need, and asked God how to choose one child. I remembered a physician I had worked for in the 1990's whose specialty was neuromuscular disorders and he was very involved with the Muscular Dystrophy Association in Memphis. His secretary had shared that Dr. Bertorini had grown up in Peru. Inspired, I selected that country and found a young girl who connected with my heart. She was wearing a dress, standing in front of the camera with her legs slightly apart and her hands on her hips. Immediately, I recalled a picture of myself in the same pose. I was four years old, wearing a light green Easter dress, and standing in front of my dad with my hands on my hips. This little girl, likewise, was four years old, and I knew without a doubt that she was the child I should sponsor.

Soon after I started this sponsorship, I received an email from Compassion about an upcoming volunteer opportunity in my area. Compassion was sponsoring the WFRN Friend Fest at Amish Acres in Nappanee on June 29th and 30th. I quickly scanned through the message and my finger was ready to click "Delete" when I heard a voice say, "You can do that." I was so stunned that I responded out loud, "HUH?" I had no interest in volunteering, but I heard the same words, "You can do that." Somewhat reluctantly, I selected the option to attend. Volunteers were especially needed for the Friday night time slot, so I signed up for that evening. As Friday afternoon approached, I was filled with uncertainty. Though I had read all the information provided, I did not have a clear idea why God wanted me to volunteer. I drove the distance of ten miles to the event in prayer and conversation with God for guidance and confidence. The familiar reassurance was present, but the fluttering persisted. As I was parking, I recognized Monica, who was getting out of the car parked next to me. We walked together towards the gate and the fluttering began to subside. The information I had received instructed me to go to the volunteer tent for my admission pass, and I recognized Pastor Jeremiah, as I approached that table. The couple in front of me was also volunteering for the Compassion event and knew where to go, so I followed them to the appropriate tent. These moments of connection were very reassuring and I was now at ease.

The music was amazing and the Compassion sponsor break was successful. As the music fest progressed, I became even more puzzled as to my role. Towards the end of the evening, I was talking with the facilitators, who had traveled from out of state to host this event. My Southern accent usually started conversations about my move to Goshen and provided opportunities to tell my stories. I shared with them my love story with Scott and my new relationship with God. As I spoke, I noticed the wife had begun to cry. Tears were streaming down her cheeks, and her husband's eyes were also full of tears. Awareness of their reaction to my stories increased as I continued to talk, and I suddenly realized the Holy Spirit was present. He was speaking to them in the spirit, while I was talking to them physically. The wife walked over to me and hugged me, still in tears, and told me that she loved me. Then I started to cry. The three of us were standing there in tears, while something amazing was going on through us and around us. She later walked me to the gate and thanked me for coming and advised me to stay close to the Lord for the next couple of days. Exhilaration and joy surged through me, as I drove out onto the highway, and I asked God out loud, "What just happened back there?" I did not hear a response, but I knew it was a

God episode. He had not sent me to just volunteer for this event; rather, He had sent me to interact with this couple.

Very early one morning in July of 2012, I woke up while I was experiencing a very warm, almost hot, sensation in the left side of my abdomen. Something astounding was happening. The heat lasted only a minute or two. I lay still on the bed, calm and at peace, during this experience. Believing I had received a miraculous healing, though I had no idea that anything was wrong, I prayed and thanked God for His blessing and protection.

I had been surprised to learn that one of the women in my grief family lived nearby. We had become good friends during the counseling and beyond those sessions. During the summer break of 2012, Patricia and I took long walks through our neighborhood on an almost daily basis, usually in the evenings. We talked and walked for hours some nights, occasionally as late as 11 p.m. We shared details about our past lives, our families and husbands, and our hopes for the future. I had a dream about my mother one night after walking with my friend. I had never dreamed about mother previously and rarely thought about her, as she had died in 1974. The dream consisted of two images. In the first picture, I was inside a close-out retail store asking a clerk if the store was closing, because their inventory was low. She was answering, "Yes" when I turned. My mother was standing there. She hugged me and was talking about work and the "Bridgewater Corporation." She was wearing a dress and her hair was long, like she had been at work. I noticed the floor was standard white tile with overhead fluorescent lighting and there were displays of general merchandise, but no name brands or store name. The picture suddenly changed. In the second image, I was in a room with a lamp on as the only light source and it was starting to storm outside. I was fiddling with the lamp and pushing against the cord. I saw a flash of lightning through the blinds. Just as I was about to knock the lamp over, I felt a hand touch me on my right shoulder from behind and I woke up. I prayed and asked God about the meaning of the dream, but received no revelation. The impression of that hand on my shoulder persisted long after I awakened.

A few nights later, I shared the dream with Patricia while we were walking, and she listened quietly as I told her about my mother's mental health history and the lack of a normal mother-daughter relationship. She suggested that I pray and thank God for the love from my mother, telling Him that I held no bad feelings towards her, and that I appreciated her love for me. Later that night, I thanked God for the love from my mother and offered forgiveness, and I asked that she be at peace. I felt a lift in my spirit after praying, and there were no further dreams about mother. My friend was a music teacher, and once school started, we were not able to continue our long late night walks. I was very thankful for this special time of friendship and healing.

Journal entry September 2011:

"The Creekside Church of the Brethren recently completed a prayer garden and labyrinth, which was featured in an article in the newspaper, open to the public. I packed a lunch today and drove to the garden for some time with the Lord, as I felt the need to be outside with Him. A wooden arbor graced the garden path entrance. Gazing up at the words carved into the arch overhead, "Bidden or Unbidden, God is Present," I understood that God is with us everywhere, always, just waiting for us to talk to Him, for the lost to call out to Him. There is no comfort or companionship that can compare to time spent alone with the Lord. I walked along the path and sat on one of the benches, soaking up the warmth of the sunshine and the beauty of the flowers and trees. A small stream flowed quietly along the walkway as well, and the gently moving water soothed my soul as I reflected on my relationship with God. Amazing blessings have been threaded through the pain and sorrow with the assurance of His constant love and His immeasurable grace. Interruptions in life come with an invitation from God, and He gives us the freedom to choose how we will respond. I was aware of increased enjoyment in regular daily activities over the past months while grieving, content to simply sit outside with a fresh cup of coffee, a book, or a writing tablet. The pleasure of those moments was enhanced by the confidence of His presence and the joy I had found in Him. Because I knew He was with me, I could relax and be at ease without thinking beyond the present. I lifted a prayer of gratitude, thanking my heavenly Father for His guidance and continued healing, and my deepening relationship with Him. I left the garden some time later with my heart and mind completely at peace. I lifted up prayers for my lost family members, as well as those of my friends. I prayed they would all accept the Lord and know Him intimately before their time ended on earth."

While putting away my dishes after dinner one evening, I dropped a glass measuring cup that shattered as it hit the floor. I was standing in front of the counter where my coffee pot was stationed when I dropped the cup. Every morning, I brewed a pot of coffee, and I was usually barefoot when I walked into the kitchen, so I wanted to be sure there were no traces of glass on the floor. I carefully cleaned up the fragments and particles, first using a broom and dustpan, next the vacuum, and then wet paper towels to capture any slivers or glass dust. Two weeks later, I made my way towards the kitchen as usual to start a pot of coffee, stopping in the doorway. A single ray of bright sunshine was streaming through the closed blind above the kitchen sink. My eyes followed this ray of light to the floor, highlighting a large single shard of glass. Joy surged through my heart. Amazed, I walked over and picked up that piece of glass. I knew I had not missed it when I cleaned the floor. I had walked barefoot in that area many times since I had broken the cup and would have stepped on this glass had it been on the floor prior to this morning. I thanked the Lord for His presence and moved through the day as usual, thanking Him again several times. Two days later, I went into the kitchen to brew my morning coffee, and again a single ray of sunshine was streaming through the blind, shining on a large single shard of glass in the same spot on the floor. Joy overflowed and I burst out laughing in the presence of the Holy Spirit. He had repeated the same steps with the piece of glass to confirm His presence and to remove any doubt. I was overjoyed by His love and assurance.

Journal entry dated 9/17/2012 at 12:17 a.m.:

"All the previous losses in my life have resurfaced with the death of Scott. I have to find myself without the familiar props I used for definition in the past—my children, my job, my activities, my possessions. God is with me. He created me and knows who I am. Have no fear."

During the Summer of 2012, my prayers included God's guidance about moving to Knoxville. I had a growing sense that I was not going to stay in Goshen, but was not sure of the timeline for moving. I did not want to repeat the sequence of events from my previous move attempt. My best friend, Anita, called me on September 18, 2012, and shared that she had dreamed about me moving the previous night. I thought I had received confirmation for the move, until I listened to a speaker on T.V. that weekend. She was talking about seeking answers from God. She said not to look for confirmation from a close friend; instead, many times, God speaks through something you read or hear, or through someone not close to you. My friend's phone call initially had seemed to confirm my prayer about moving, but now doubts crowded my thoughts. I prayed again for God's direction. I told Him I would not keep asking, and if I did not hear from Him clearly, I would stay in Goshen.

My job underwent several changes after Scott's death, but I remained employed. I received a book, Jesus Calling, along with a devotional booklet of the same name on September 28, 2012, from a woman in Memphis named Mary, whom I had met recently through my job. Our work required that we communicate several times a day by email. One day, she asked some personal questions, and I responded with details about my marriage and Scott's sudden death and my continued employment from this distance. She was kind and sympathetic, sharing words of encouragement and friendship. Her husband asked her why she was sending these books to a woman she barely knew, and she explained that she was following the prompting of the Holy Spirit.

I was touched by her thoughtfulness and started reading the book during my quiet time. The day after praying about moving, I was reading the devotion booklet on Day 9, and God spoke to me through the words confirming the decision to move.

I shared with Mary that my sister and I had grown up in the Annesdale-Snowden Historic District in Memphis and had attended the neighborhood schools. She asked if we had attended Central Baptist Church, because it was located in the same area. Startled by her question, I explained that we did, until the church moved out of Midtown, while we were in our teens and were no longer able to attend. Her husband's family had attended there for many years, and he had kept copies of the older church directories. She found our picture that was taken in the 1970's and emailed a copy. Mary also mailed a copy of the entire church directory. I did not remember this picture of my sister and me, and I felt a twinge of joy mixed with deep sadness, as I looked at that old image, recalling the days when I was saved and baptized. I remembered the Bible stories and Jesus songs—a sanctuary in a chaotic, unhappy childhood.

I also recalled two older ladies, perhaps sisters, who lived on Minna Place in the same neighborhood where I grew up, a short distance from the church. They had a swing set with wooden seats in the backyard, which I loved, because I could stand on the seat to start swinging and then sit down. These women held a Bible class in their home once a week after school. We would listen to a Bible story or watch a film, sing songs, and then work on a craft project downstairs at tables set up in the basement. I loved going there, because I always felt safe and welcome. The women were sweet and gentle in nature. They both wore navy blue dresses, dark shoes from the 1940's, and glasses. One of them had short gray curly hair. I could not remember their names, but had gone to their house many times prior to the picture that was taken for the church directory. One of the craft projects involved cutting out clothes for a Donna Reed paper doll. Another time, we cut out and pasted scenes into a Bible story picture. At Christmas, they gave us a roll of LifeSavers. I wanted to remember more about these women, but the memories were more like flash images. I assumed they attended Central Baptist Church, but I did not find their pictures in the church directory.

After receiving confirmation from God about moving, my sole concern about the time frame required for the move was my job. My employment had recently gone through another transition, and I was not sure how I was going to handle packing and moving, while maintaining my work responsibilities. My workload was heavy, and I would have to be offline four days for this move. Incredibly, I was given the option of direct deposit, eliminating any worry about a lost check during my move. Two weeks before the move, I learned that my employer would be out of town during the same time frame that I would be offline. I was tremendously relieved with the work pressure removed, and I thanked God for those timely and unexpected blessings.

I found a suitable place to live rather quickly, a townhouse in a great location that was affordable, and approval came within two days. Another round began of sorting, packing, and donating, with more boxes, bubble wrap, and tape.

I had held onto Scott's chess set following his death. He had treasured the memories of past games and had shared stories involving those friends. He had remained friends after graduation and through adulthood with Bill, who was also our insurance agent. I had not met him, but knew that his friendship was special to Scott. As I prepared to pack the chess set, I was filled with the suggestion to give it to Bill. The idea persisted, and I set the chess set aside, while I continued to pack. I later phoned the office where Bill worked and set up an appointment to meet him and discuss transferring insurance coverage to the State of Tennessee.

I was at peace with my decision to give Bill the chess set as I drove to his office for our meeting. Though he had attended Scott's funeral, I had not been introduced to him. I was glad to finally connect a face to his name from the memories Scott had shared previously. He told of some adventures from their younger years, and we laughed in remembrance of our beloved Scott. During our conversation, I sensed that Bill was curious about our meeting and relationship. I may not have been the type of woman Scott would have been attracted to in his youth, but Scott had become a changed man. Those who had known Scott for many years tended to view him through eyes of the past, whereas I knew him as the man he had become, and I looked at him differently. Curious, I asked Bill how Scott had remained unattached, since he was an attractive man with good qualities. He explained that Scott was unique in that if he was not interested, nothing could grab his interest, regardless of who or what was trying to get his attention. He said something in me must have fascinated Scott to have captured and held his attention. I reassured Bill that I loved his lifelong friend with all my heart and was blessed to have been his wife. I presented him with the chess set and explained that I wanted him to have it in honor of their shared memories during Scott's life. Bill was very appreciative of the gift, and I was thankful for the opportunity to meet and talk with Scott's close friend.

I met with my grief family on October 20, 2012 for our monthly fellowship. They wanted to recognize my birthday, so we met at a new restaurant downtown where the mood was warm and intimate. After praying over our meal, Beverley instructed us to save the paper strip wrapped around our silverware for later. We enjoyed our food, and after dinner we rode to Bev's house for dessert and conversation. We shared some cake and the group gave me a card they had all signed. Then Bev asked everyone to take their paper strip and write some words about me on the paper, and in turn, I was to write a few words about all of them on my strip. She gathered the strips and read them out loud. I was deeply moved by their words and affection. This group had been a blessing to me over the last thirteen months, and I was suddenly apprehensive about letting go of their support. We had encouraged each other through our significant anniversaries and birthdays, as well as the holidays, and I sadly informed them that I would be moving to Knoxville the next month. They all offered encouragement and prayers for my new beginning.

During the past year, I had attended a discipleship class that met every week under the leadership of Monica. This had been an intense study, sometimes with a heavy homework burden. I wondered many times if I had taken on more than I could handle with my ongoing grief. Monica had continued to encourage me throughout the course, and I finished the class with a sense of accomplishment. The other woman in our group, Sylvia, invited Monica and me for dinner at her home on Tuesday, October 30th. The three of us had grown closer in our relationship during the study, and soon I would no longer see these dear women. The food was delicious, and I enjoyed our last meal together, though it was bittersweet in light of my upcoming move.

Sue dropped by on Friday, November 2nd, for a quick visit. We shared hugs and tears, as I updated her on the details of my plans. Just before leaving, she handed me a card, but would not allow me to open it until after she left. The front of the card displayed a picture of us taken during one of our meetings at "The Electric Brew." Inside the card was another picture of us, taken by one of the baristas, while we were sitting at a table talking over coffee. Tears flowed with those memories and I read her words in amazement.

"They say nothing happens by accident. I like to say nothing happens except when God is involved. I had just come through a difficult year fighting breast cancer and had no idea that the following year would be even harder.

Enter....You. My heart ached when I saw you at Scott's funeral with your two adult children who would be going home the next week. My heart ached when I thought about you alone without the man you loved more than anything in this world.

Enter....Jesus. He knew I would need a friend who could speak with wisdom and love straight into my soul. You were grieving, I was hurting, and your faith carried me through many hard weeks. Yes, it was about you and I loved learning about your past, your dreams, your love story, and your deep sorrow. But God knew I needed your words. It was as if God Himself was speaking to me and I wept many times. You did not even know that you were ministering to me, but you were. Iris, you were indeed Jesus with skin on.

Enter....Peace. I am sad to see you go, but so excited for how God will continue to use you and guide you and give you peace. My heart is at peace, your heart is at peace, and it started in a little coffee shop in Goshen.

Blessings to you my friend,

Love you,
Sue"

I redirected my thoughts to moving preparations. On the day I secured the rental of a moving truck, Monica met me off site to drive the truck back to my place. I was not confident behind the wheel of this large vehicle. She had driven similar trucks many times and had graciously offered to drive and back the twenty-two foot rental truck into my driveway. Movers arrived to load the truck the next morning. The following day, Monica returned with her sister and brothers to help with the last minute clean-up. She stayed behind when the others left to help me stuff my vehicle with everything that would not pack in a box. While we were working that night, my grief family dropped by for a surprise visit. They brought some cake, many hugs, and much love to say goodbye. I was going to miss these familiar faces. My father-in-law had found a man that I had employed to drive the truck, and all the moving arrangements had been finalized. My son would meet me once I arrived in Knoxville and would help me get settled. After Monica and my friends left, I sat on the floor of my empty living room in quiet solitude. I planned to sleep on the floor and get up early the next morning to drive to Tennessee.

I settled down for the evening and thought about all the changes in my life over just a few short years. The most important change was my relationship with God and the tremendous spiritual growth I had experienced through this deep valley of hurt and loss. When the pain took my breath away, His presence brought reassurance. During the darkest longest nights, He comforted me with His peace. I started crying at the thought of leaving behind all that had become familiar, and then I was reminded of all the past blessings from God, as I prepared for the night. I knew without any doubt that God loved me more than I could comprehend and that He would never abandon me. I trusted Him. He would be with me and love me forever.

Chapter Nine

BLESSINGS REVISITED

As I revisited the blessings of God's intervention in my life in the past, my spirit was humbled with overflowing gratitude.

God had changed my life through the love from Scott. Through smiles and tears, I mentally reviewed all of the beautiful love touches from my relationship with him. Never had anyone displayed such affection for me and a desire for my happiness. My gift giving had paled in comparison to his wonderful surprises. I felt a twinge of guilt over my lack of creativity in that area. I had talked to God about this one night during my quiet time, and He had revealed that Scott had not wanted me to compete--he only wanted my gratitude.

God reminded me of the times I was alone as a child, yet never harmed. My sister and I walked to and from school every day through all of our school years, and we had to walk on a very busy thoroughfare with a heavy flow of commercial traffic. We learned at an early age that stop, look, and listen applied to both the activity on the sidewalk and the moving traffic. As we matured into our teens, we were alert to any cars that might slow down and follow us, as we walked along the sidewalk. I ignored any men offering rides or shouting obscenities from passing car windows, refusing to turn my head or look at the drivers. I was not jumped, attacked, or harmed in any way during all those years in school. During our grade school years, Officer Frank Stotts was stationed at the one busy intersection we had to maneuver every day to help us cross the street safely. He was kind, and his presence was reassuring. I looked forward to seeing him on school days and eagerly showed him my report card each six week period in anticipation of his encouraging words. He retired before I entered the sixth grade. I remembered him with fondness and thanked God for his presence at that intersection every day while we were young children walking to elementary school.

God had kept me safe when my sister pulled a gun on me as a child. We were with our dad on a visit to Aunt Ora's farm in Arkansas. He was talking to Uncle Fred, while my sister and I played outside in the yard. The trunk of the car was open, as we had arrived shortly before and had not yet taken our bags into the house. My sister started looking around in the trunk and found the gun my dad always carried when he traveled. She called my name and pointed it at me. While everyone was yelling at her, I was running as fast as my ten-year-old legs would carry me into the house. The gun was not fired and I was safe.

God had protected my sister and me during those summers when we traveled to and from Texas to visit our dad. On the first trip we flew back to Memphis, but all subsequent travel was by bus. I made most of those trips alone, including the trip to and from Little Rock to visit my mother. The bus ride from Texas to Memphis seemed endless, stopping in many small towns where I had to exit the bus at some stations for varying intervals of time. I was not harmed or bothered during any of these stops, even when traveling through the early morning hours, although sometimes, I was afraid when men would notice me or look at me too long. I felt vulnerable on those trips when I was alone, but God had kept me safe without any incidents.

God had protected me from drugs and alcohol. I was so shy and timid and on the straight and narrow path that no one offered me any drugs during my years in junior high or high school. I was labeled a goody two shoes and was not invited to parties. I had no desire for alcohol, because of what I had seen in my father and stepmother and others who drank. Drinking brought the ugly out of the people I was exposed to under the influence, and I did not want to be like them. I had been afraid of drugs. The police had come to our elementary school and talked about drug use and its effects on the body. I was shocked and disturbed at pictures they showed of addicts. Everyone in my family, including my parents and aunt, smoked cigarettes. I would get car sick while riding with my aunt with the windows closed. I detested the smell of cigarettes and never had any interest in smoking. I believe God provided the lack of desire for those things for my own good, and I was very grateful for His protection.

God had blessed me as a mother to a precious son and daughter. I remembered my excitement when I was pregnant with our first child, honored to become a mother and somewhat nervous about the labor and delivery. One day at work, a coworker commented that she was concerned about me becoming a mother, because I had no mother and would not know how to love my child. Her words shocked me, and I was unbelievably hurt by her assessment. The love came naturally with my children and my husband. In spite of a lack of love growing up, I was affectionate with others and told my children I loved them every day. I hugged and kissed my babies and was very blessed through my husband and children.

God had blessed my first marriage in spite of the very rocky beginning. As a mother, I had not been obedient in taking my children to church. They attended after school care at a local church, but that was no substitute. I had wanted their father to attend with us as a family, but he had no interest in church, and his job required that he work some weekends. I could have taken them alone, but failed to do so, because of my insecurity and severe shyness. I was uncomfortable talking to strangers and meeting new people. I felt socially awkward around other mothers. The rejection from childhood continued to affect my self-image and my confidence.

God had saved my daughter and me through her very difficult birth. During the delivery, she became lodged in the birth canal, and it was too late for a C-section. Delivery was imperative at that moment. In an effort to save my daughter, the doctor grabbed her arm and pulled her out. I was totally unaware of this while it was happening in the delivery room. I heard her expectant cry and thanked God for her life. The nurses gave her a good newborn report; however, the left hand was normally positioned close to her face, but her right arm was lying limp on her chest. The doctor explained that in order to save her life as well as mine, they had to pull her out by her arm, and only time would tell if the arm would develop normally. There was a 50/50 possibility that her arm would never develop to full size, and it would be months before we would know if the arm was damaged permanently. We were referred to a pediatric neurologist for further evaluation, and it became a wait-and-see scenario. The skin was warm with good color, but only time would tell. We were advised not to exercise the arm and to bring her back for a repeat evaluation in a few months. I prayed regularly for God's healing. She was a happy, healthy baby otherwise, and I was thankful for our daughter. At the next doctor evaluation, there were signs the arm was healthy, and we were given instructions on simple maneuvers to perform with her arm until the next visit. After several months, the doctor determined that the arm was developing normally without limitation or deformity, and we were released from his care. God had answered my prayers.

God had protected me from the threat of evil. I was required to maintain the yard at the house where the children and I were living after the divorce. Spring was on its way, and the grass was beginning to grow. While I was standing outside one afternoon thinking about the yard and no lawnmower and no money to purchase yard equipment, a man came walking down the street pushing a lawnmower and carrying a small gas can. He asked if I needed the yard mowed, and we agreed on a fee. We never spoke on the phone; he just showed up when the yard needed to be cut, and I paid him when he finished. I was not completely at ease with this man, and I limited our conversation to the yard work. I did not stay outside while he worked and maintained eye contact with him every time we spoke. Late one night, in the middle of summer, we were awakened by loud knocking at the front door. My children and I gathered in the living room in apprehension. I yelled through the locked door and asked who was knocking. A voice replied it was the yard man. I yelled back that I did not need any yard work at midnight and there was nothing here for him. I began praying fervently for protection for my children and myself. I stood there in silence with my arms around my children and waited, still praying. He left at that point. I thanked God for keeping us safe.

God had saved my life. I recall the day back in the late 1990's, while driving to work on the interstate in pouring rain at 60 mph in my truck, when I hydroplaned off the interstate, totally out of my control, down a steep embankment. I was holding onto the steering wheel looking ahead, not accelerating, when suddenly my truck veered off the road over the shoulder, as though someone else was driving. I spun around and around, sliding downward over the grassy surface, until I came to a stop in front of a concrete culvert. Everything had happened very quickly. My first words when the truck stopped moving were, "Thank God I'm alive." I sat in the truck trying to grasp what had just happened and thanking God repeatedly. When I got out assessing any damage to my vehicle, there was no scratch or dent on the truck. I was completely unharmed.

God had given me comfort and reassurance in my loneliness and fear. He reminded me of the time I was in the hospital at age fifteen. I had a history of ear infections with hearing loss and had failed the school hearing test for two years. The doctor was going to perform surgery to repair my eardrum and replace a tiny ear bone that had deteriorated. He explained this was probably due to an untreated ear infection during infancy. My aunt was with me during the admission process and left the hospital once I was assigned to a semi-private room. An older teen who had been involved in a severe motorcycle accident occupied the bed by the window, and I was next to the door. A nurse came in frequently to perform suction on the young woman, and I shuddered every time I heard those sounds, as she moaned in protest. She had a steady stream of family and friends who came to visit every day. In contrast, no one was with me, and no one came to see me. I felt conspicuously alone, as her visitors walked by my bed. I had been afraid when I looked in the mirror and saw my head bandaged the day after surgery, but I had felt a soft reassurance in spite of my fear and loneliness. God revealed that He had been with me and reminded me that the surgery was successful without any complications.

God had saved my life more than once. I had returned to my previous job in 2000 and was commuting about 160 miles round trip every workday. I also worked overtime many days and even weekends when the work volume required. The travel had become exhausting after several months. On this afternoon, fatigue set in early during the drive home. Approximately eight to ten miles from home, my energy level completely bottomed out, and I nodded off. I prayed for help to make it home safely. Struggling to stay awake, I nodded off once more. Suddenly, my head jerked up, and in the middle of the interstate ahead was a large German Shepherd. This dog was standing still, straddling the two lanes, with his head turned towards my truck. Instantly, I was wide awake. Thankfully there were no vehicles around me, as I slammed hard on the brakes. The dog then trotted off the roadway and quickly disappeared in my rear view mirror, as I drove in the opposite direction. God had protected me, as well as other drivers from harm.

God had protected my health and body. My insurance coverage had lapsed between job changes and I was not financially able to pay the Cobra premium during that time. As a result, once I was insured again, an eighteen month preexisting clause was held against me. During this span of time, I did not see my doctor for regular checkups. My monthly cycles had always been irregular, often missing one or two months between periods in my 20's and 30's. When my period ceased for thirteen months, I assumed that I was in early menopause, as I was approaching forty years of age. After the eighteen month delay passed, I was able to visit my previous gynecologist for the overdue check-up. He was alarmed when I shared that thirteen months had passed since my last menstrual cycle. Though I had not been sexually active, pregnancy was ruled out per protocol. He explained that I needed to have a period at least every quarter and assured me I was not in early menopause. Feeling somewhat dismayed at this information, I was embarrassed over the lack of knowledge about my own body. He prescribed Provera for a few days to trigger a period and warned me that I would have a very heavy flow, as the uterine lining had built up every month, though it had not been discharged. He also drew a blood hormone profile. He explained that once my menstrual flow stopped, I would need to return for a D&C for a biopsy. I was surprised by his concern and the plan of treatment, but I agreed to return for the procedure. At my return visit two weeks later, he reviewed the results of the hormone profile with me. He said my hormones were so out of order he was amazed that I had been able to conceive a second child. I was stunned at that information, as my daughter was now a young child. He tried to obtain a sample for biopsy in the office, but was unsuccessful, necessitating a visit to the one-day surgery center for the D&C. The results were negative, and follow-up pap smears were normal. God had blessed me with my precious daughter and had kept me healthy; while I was unaware there was anything wrong in my body. I was humbled at this revelation and thankful for His amazing love and compassion.

God had provided favor and had protected my employment. I had shared with the office administrator all of the pertinent details of my plans to move to Indiana soon after the first of the year in January of 2008. Scott and I had agreed that once I was settled into our new home, I could start searching for a job in Goshen. In the meantime, his salary would cover our needs. Unbelievably, the administrator called me several days later with a proposal to continue working for the office as an independent contractor, rather than an employee. This was totally unexpected. At that time, no one who was employed by that office worked at home. The administrator authorized the IT Department to reprogram my computer for remote use and to download all the necessary software for access to the system from Indiana. IT also provided backup program software in case of a computer crash, as well as contact information for support. We negotiated a line count fee versus an hourly rate with the understanding that I would bill the office every two weeks following the same payroll cycle. I left the office, after ten years of employment, with my computer including the monitor, keyboard, mouse, foot pedal, and printer, as well as my office chair to take with me to Indiana. I was stunned at this development just before I moved, never dreaming of the possibility to remain employed with this office. God had worked in a wondrous way, and He continued to protect my employment following Scott's death through several major changes in the office.

God had provided assistance many times previously in my life. I re-lived the happiest moments, the years my children were growing up and my marriage to Scott, as well as the many difficult situations where God worked through strangers, extending back to childhood. I was reminded of one experience in particular in June of 2000. While driving home from an auction in Arkansas on a secondary highway, I had a flat. I had not previously changed a tire on my vehicle, and apprehension grew as I pulled onto the shoulder. I turned on my flashers and removed the manual from the glove compartment. I located the spare tire mounted under the vehicle and lowered it onto the ground. Unfortunately, the rim had rusted onto the bracket holding the tire and I tried, unsuccessfully, to knock it loose with a tire iron. Frustrated and a little worried, I got back into my van and shut the door. I kept the windows closed, because I was surrounded by fields of crops, the insects were thick, and I did not want my vehicle full of bugs. It was almost dark at this point. I knew the next exit was at least five miles down the road, and I was not going to walk along the highway alone at night. I prayed, but somehow I knew help was not going to come soon. I had no cell phone and no one to call. I cranked the engine every so often for fresh air. No one stopped, and the sun yielded to the night sky. The local traffic soon died down, until no more tail lights passed by. I dozed off and on through the night, cranking the engine for fresh air each time I woke up. I had decided when daylight broke I would start walking. I fell asleep sometime after midnight and woke up again around 6 a.m. The sun was rising. I opened the door and stepped out to stretch. Just at that moment, a Yellow Freight truck stopped on the opposite side of the highway. The driver ran across the road and kindly asked if I needed any help. He said he would be glad to change the tire for me. When I offered to pay him, he refused any money and asked if I went to church. I answered that I attended sometimes. He told me the next time I went to church to just drop something extra in the plate. I gave him a hug and noticed the name patch on his shirt read "Thomas." I cried driving home, overwhelmed with emotion and tremendously relieved. God had sent a stranger to my rescue once again, as He had so many times in the past.

Over the next week, I kept thinking about Thomas and how I wished I could do something to thank him personally. The idea popped into my mind to write a letter to Yellow Freight. Every time I started thinking about the letter, though, something would distract me and I would put it off. The prompting to follow through persisted, and I finally composed a letter via the Yellow Freight website, praying it would find its way to the appropriate recipient. I received a response the next morning from a department director thanking me for the letter and asking for my permission to use it in their company publication. In addition, Thomas was going to receive a commendation for his courtesy and kindness. The message explained Thomas' surprise when he was called into the office and shown my letter. He was astonished that I had taken the time to write the company. I was thrilled he received that recognition and felt guilty for not writing sooner.

For years I had viewed that incident as God coming to my rescue, but for the first time, I revisited that night from a different perspective. I recalled that I had not been hungry or thirsty throughout the night, and I had not needed to use the bathroom. I had also been somewhat surprised that no one had stopped. What if God wanted to bless Thomas, and I was the vessel He used to deliver the blessing? The realization was very humbling and opened my eyes a little wider. I prayed God's blessing on Thomas and all the strangers who had helped me through the years, and I thanked God for His immeasurable love and grace.

Chapter Ten

NO WHITE PICKET FENCES

I did not remember ever feeling loved or wanted as a child. I grew up in a time when most children had intact families and lived with both parents. My sister and I have no memories of living with our parents, as they divorced before I was four years old and she was barely two. Our mother's behavior radically changed at some point after the birth of my younger sister. She was committed to a hospital and subsequently diagnosed with paranoid schizophrenia. Our father worried about our safety as well as his after the diagnosis. The doctor did not think she would hurt us, but warned my father not to turn his back on her. We never lived with our mother after the divorce. While she was in the hospital, we lived with one of her brothers and his family in the country. I did not remember any love from those people. Sometime later, we were sent to a foster family in another city, and my aunt and uncle kept all of our clothes, except the dresses we were wearing the day we left their house. This new family had boys, and we wore their hand-me-down t-shirts and jeans that were cut off for shorts. We played outside all day and slept on a divan in a front bedroom alone. We sat on the floor in the living room to watch T.V., while the family sat on the couch. We didn't go anywhere with them in the car.

One day, our father came for a visit and treated us with an ice cream cone. Afterwards, he had to take us back to that house, and I cried and cried when he drove away. I wanted so desperately to go with him, as I had been waiting every day for him to come and take us home. Dad explained he could not take us yet, but that he would be back soon. Finally, one day, Aunt Lucy arrived in her Chrysler and packed us up and took us back to Texas. I was so happy, glad to leave these strangers, and excited to see Dad again.

Our father had remarried while we were living outside the home. Our stepmother made it clear she was not sharing our father and was not interested in raising his two little girls. They argued about us constantly. Our father never missed work, but he drank on the weekends and sometimes at night. Our stepmother drank beer during the day, while Dad was at work. He provided the money that paid all the bills, and she stayed at home to keep house, cook, and take care of us. We were forced to play outside during the daytime, and we looked for other kids to play with in the neighborhood. On rainy days, she sent us outside as soon as the rain stopped. Anything was better than being in the house with her and listening to the soap operas that she watched on T.V. all day. When Dad came home from work, we would run outside to see him and hug him, but our stepmother would order us to go play in the backyard. If he disagreed with her, another argument would start, sometimes developing into a full-blown fight with cursing, throwing things, and neighbors coming outside to view the mayhem. Dad was going to buy a newspaper one Saturday and asked us if we wanted to ride with him to the store. We squealed in excitement, as we ran outside behind him, scrambling onto the front seat next to him. Suddenly, my stepmother yanked the car door open and ordered us to get into the back seat. She looked at us with cold, dark eyes and pointing toward her chest said, "I come first." Then pointing at us, she said, "You come second." We rode to the store in silence, the time with Dad now spoiled by her presence and her words.

One night, the fighting and cursing escalated, and my stepmother began throwing things out the front door. Glass shattered on the concrete porch and steps, and spread to the front walk out to the sidewalk. As the fight moved into the front yard, neighbors began to gather. Dad took my sister and me by the hand, and we started running down the sidewalk. We walked slowly around a long block and returned to the house. Dad got the car and took us to dinner. When we drove home later in the evening, our stepmother had bolted the doors and locked the windows. Dad busted the front door to get in, and they argued throughout the remainder of the night. Sometimes, the police were called. I was ashamed and embarrassed when the neighbors witnessed their behavior. We moved around town frequently due to the fighting. A brother and sister lived across the street in one neighborhood and played with us outside, but we were not allowed in their house. I was acutely aware of how people reacted to my sister and me.

When the fighting continued unceasing to a breaking point, my father would drive us back to Memphis to Aunt Lucy's house and leave us there, without any warning or advance notice. I never knew what was going to happen from one day to the next. My father did what he thought was best for his situation, without regard for how this was affecting us. I looked around at other children and thought about Jesus who loved all of us, because He created us. It seemed to me that He loved other children more than me, because they had parents and families. They played together, went places together, and loved one another. My sister and I had not experienced any of these things. We were not loved or wanted, and we did not fit anywhere.

I was allowed to start school at age five, because my birthday was in October. During the first grade, I attended three different schools in three different states. One teacher wrote on my report card that I was being affected emotionally by the constant moving and advised a stable home environment. I began having blackout spells when the fighting intensified between my father and stepmother. I could not stand the yelling, the constant rejection, and the uncertainty of what might be going on at home when I walked home from school every day. My sister began wetting the bed around age three. For punishment, my stepmother put a diaper on her and made her ride her tricycle up and down the street on the sidewalk, while dad was at work. One night, they made her sit in the living room without any pants, while we had company. She sat there trying desperately to stretch her top down long enough to cover herself. Sometimes, Dad would take us to the park to play or swim in the public pool. He pushed the swings and caught us at the bottom of the slippery slides. I would yell for him to push me higher, until I squealed with the bounce of the swing. The trips to the park offered a short sweet reprieve from life at home. I felt safe with Dad when our stepmother was not around. She never smiled or laughed or participated as a family. She was cruel and cold, while Dad was charming and attractive. I did not understand why he loved her and why he did not protect us from her.

Eventually, Dad chose her over us, and he left us at Aunt Lucy's house in Memphis for the last time. I was beginning second grade and my sister was starting kindergarten. Our aunt provided a stable home without any drinking or fighting, but there was no love. She had never had any children of her own and was now in her 50's. We lived in a grand old house, but there was no warmth. I would lie in my bed at night crying, looking out the window at the top of the streetlight that glowed brightly throughout the night, and I would ask God why I couldn't have just one normal parent? Why couldn't I have someone who loved me, who wanted me?

I heard about Jesus at Sunday school as a young child. How I loved the Bible studies and songs! There was no love or affection at home, and I wanted to hear about this man who loved me. I would sing the songs I learned in Sunday school, while walking to school or playing at home or sitting in the porch swing. Singing those songs brought a measure of comfort, easing the sadness and loneliness. Church provided escape for a few precious years. I was allowed to go on retreats and take field trips to amusement parks and campgrounds with the church groups. I enjoyed those times, because I felt normal and happy when I was away from home. When asked at church about my family, I quickly learned it was a mistake to share the truth about my parents. I had talked about my mother and her illness, as well as life with my dad and stepmother. I was shunned and avoided by many of the church people, who gave their attention to the children with parents who attended and supported the church. I was looking for someone to listen and reassure me that Jesus really did love me, but the adults would just turn away without saying anything. I sensed that my presence made them uncomfortable, and I tried to understand their reaction. There must be something wrong with me. I had been taught that the church was God's house and those who belong to the church are God's people. How could God love me when I was not accepted by His people in His house?

There were two women at that neighborhood Baptist church, Mrs. Gregory and Ms. Newman, who made a lasting impression on my heart with their kindness and love. They arranged for me to attend summer camp for a couple of years through the church. Summer camp was the most fun I had experienced up to that point. Kids came to this camp from all over, and most were strangers. I felt a deep sense of relief with the realization that I could be myself and would not have to talk about my parents and family. The days were filled with hiking, swimming, games,

Bible stories, songs, fellowship, and fun. I never wanted to go home. Ms. Newman drove me to the camp and then returned to take me back home at the end of the week. I later discovered that the women's auxiliary at the church had paid the cost of the camp, and these two women served on the board. I wrote them a note thanking them for their generosity.

My church relocated during my early teens to another part of the city. I was no longer able to attend, as I had no transportation. This was a heavy loss. My sister had stopped going to church a few years prior, and my aunt attended a Methodist church. There was no other church in the neighborhood. I was saved and baptized at that church when I was twelve-years-old. I had walked forward during the invitation and was baptized by the pastor a few weeks later in front of the church, wearing a white robe. I felt like a different person when I was lifted out of the water. No one in my family was there to witness this wonderful moment in my life, but I was proud of myself for obeying God. I did not always understand what the preacher was saying, but I loved singing the old hymns as part of the congregation. Something happened when I sang those old verses. My heart would fill with emotion, and I would cry in release. It was a wonderful feeling and my favorite part of the service. The church's relocation out of the neighborhood left a huge void in my life.

Aunt Lucy also changed when I hit my early teens. She became even more unhappy, critical, and depressed. I did not know if it was related to her age, as she was now in her 60's, or if our presence in the house was a source of conflict between our aunt and uncle. He was not involved in our care or daily lives. For several years, he lived in Beaumont and came home for short visits every few months. They slept in separate bedrooms and did not appear to communicate much with each other. We were not allowed to talk at the dinner table when he was home. I never understood their relationship, but they were married for over fifty years, until his death.

She would become irritable and argumentative over trivial things. I tried to avoid her at those times, because I did not want to disrespect her, and it was a challenge to be civil. When she would start yelling at me, I would walk away from her and head upstairs to my room. She would follow me, shouting at my back, as I climbed the steps, "You're going to be crazy just like your mother." I would mutter under my breath with each step, "No, I'm Not. No, I'm Not. No, I'm Not." Though I rejected her words, deep down, I carried this fear for many, many years. I was constantly reminded that I looked exactly like my mother. Whenever my sister and I were around other relatives, everyone commented on how much we had grown since they last saw us, followed by the same comparisons--that my sister looked like our dad and I looked like our mother. The fear that I would become like my mother grew every time I heard those words.

I was a good student in school and strived to make good grades. Though not appreciated by others, my report card gave me a sense of achievement. I was not a problem child, and as a young teen, I was not involved in partying, drinking, or experimenting with drugs. I taught myself to sew in junior high school and developed a love for reading. One summer in particular, I made many walking trips to the public library, which was more than a mile from home. I carried a large shopping bag, alternating hands several times during the long walk. Instead of taking a direct route along the main streets, I wandered through different neighborhoods of the houses that I liked, noticing the yards, trees, flowers, and architecture, adding distance to my walk. I would linger at the library, carefully choosing my next bag of books to read and then start my journey home, again meandering through different neighborhoods and creating my own adventure, enjoying the time spent outside of the chaotic atmosphere in the house. We lived in a good neighborhood, and there were other kids to play with outside. As a young child, I would play dolls, do crafts, or listen to a portable radio on the porch. I learned to roller skate on the porch, gradually venturing out to the sidewalk. I also liked to climb trees and ride my bicycle.

In my tween and early teen years, our aunt started sending my sister and me to spend part of the summer with other relatives. The first trip was to Texas to spend two weeks with our dad and stepmother. As soon as we arrived and were settled in, my aunt called and told my father to keep us that we could just stay there and live, and he could see what it was like to raise his kids. This was a pattern repeated over the next couple of years between my father and his sister. When Aunt Lucy first took us into her home, she thought it was only going to be temporary. When I started school for the second year, however, the principal informed her that she would have to obtain custody to keep us in school. My aunt took my sister with her to juvenile court to start custody proceedings. The judge ruled that my sister and I had been through too much, and that if my aunt wanted the younger child, she would have to take the older child as well. She was granted custody, and that caused a major rift in her relationship with my father for many years. He sent a check every week for support and an allowance for my sister and me along with a letter. We had to write him back, or he would get upset and call my aunt wanting to know why we had not written. She did not want the money to stop, so we wrote him back every Sunday night, and she mailed it the next day. The check and letter from Dad faithfully arrived every Friday.

The next year when we visited Dad during the summer, our step-mother decided to make us something special to wear. She had become more civil towards us now that we were older and the threat of having to raise us had been removed. She was an excellent seamstress and made her own clothes. She had made our dresses during the time we lived with them as young children. For me, she chose to construct a jacket of double-knit material, which was very popular in the 1970's, lining it and trimming it in navy blue. The jacket body was a patchwork of stitched squares of different patterns and colors. I was dismayed when she proudly showed me the finished project, because it looked more appro-priate for an older woman. I was only fifteen at the time, and I knew I would not wear this jacket once I returned home. I thanked her with as much enthusiasm as I could muster. For my sister, she constructed a long, red gown that could be worn to a school dance or a prom. I thought it was beautiful and looked very good on my sister. I could not help but wonder why she did not make a dress like this for me, instead of the old lady jacket. Why was I always treated differently?

The only time I saw Aunt Lucy happy was when we had company or when visiting her family or friends. She enjoyed sharing stories from the past and would laugh and smile often during those visits. She viewed life as a battle, and some of those battles involved other people who lived on our street. She referred to most of our neighbors as ol' man or ol' lady so-and-so, and she would speak her own assessment of each neighbor when she saw them. She summed up the whole world from the front porch. One such battle involved ol' man Goodman and his dog doing its busi-ness in our yard. Somehow, she had determined that his dog was the culprit, though many of our neighbors walked their dogs every afternoon and stopped in the same yards. She sat in wait on the porch one after-noon as ol' man Goodman and his dog made their way along the sidewalk towards our house. His dog stopped in our yard, and she was off the swing in a flash in full battle mode. Failing to get a word in edgewise, the poor man turned around and shuffled back down the sidewalk, mumbling under his breath. After that day, he walked his dog in the opposite direction of our house.

There was a girl who lived with her grandparents further down our street. I did not know her family circumstances, as my sister and I had only played with her outside a few times. One day, she came to our house with her mother, who informed my aunt that my sister and I had taken her daughter's doll, and she had come to get it back. We were called to the front door and questioned about the doll. We explained that we had not taken any of her toys. My aunt set her straight and shut the door. We were ordered to stay away from the girl, as she did not want that mother to ever step foot on her porch again.

My aunt had bought her house in the 1960's, and by the 1980's it was designated as part of an historic district. Built in 1912, the house measured approximately 3000 square feet with four bedrooms upstairs. Several elderly women on the street rented some of the extra bedrooms in their homes. Our neighbor on one side rented several rooms and the basement. Unfortunately, her back yard was small, which did not allow much room for vehicles to maneuver in and out of the driveway. The residents had started using our backyard to back up and turn around. This was tearing up the grass, and after an unsuccessful discussion with the neighbor, my aunt had a chain link fence installed. She was visited years later by a representative of the neighborhood association and asked to remove the fence in keeping with the aesthetics of the time period for the neighborhood. This issue was of no concern to my aunt, and the fence remained as long as she lived in the house. Thankfully, their attention was diverted when a resident the next street over painted their front porch red. My aunt had strong opinions about a group telling her what she could and could not do to her own property.

The most heated battles centered on our father and stepmother. We had told our aunt about the cruelty from our stepmother, the fighting, and the moving. She had been angry with Dad and had confronted him on the phone, but he denied what we said and believed that our aunt had put ideas in our head.

One Christmas, our stepmother's sister gave my sister and me a pretty homemade stool with nice fabric and trim, using metal coffee cans. I was delighted with the gift and appreciative of her kindness and generosity. Aunt Lucy was livid when we brought the stools home after we told her who had given them to us. She loaded the stools into the car and told us to get in as well. Lucy drove over to this couple's home, which was about twenty-five miles from our house, and parked on the street. She opened the trunk and tossed the stools into the front yard, and I was heartbroken, as they rolled over through the grass and dirt. I was upset that I could not keep the gift and embarrassed and ashamed of her behavior. We returned home in strained silence. She was angry that we had accepted this gift in light of our feelings towards our stepmother. Our aunt found it difficult to forgive anyone who hurt her, and that included us. She viewed our enjoyment of time spent with our dad as betrayal to her, and her words and behavior punished us long after any interaction with our father. She would remind us of how we were treated when we lived with him and then get angry that we still loved him and wanted to see him. Her words were hurtful and unforgiving.

The worst part about living with our aunt was the renters who lived in the house. She had run a boarding house in the past and when we came to live with her, she was still renting out the extra bedrooms upstairs, though not providing meals. The renters were all male, of different ages. My sister and I had been sharing the small breakfast room downstairs off the kitchen, but as we grew older, we needed more space. When I turned twelve, our aunt finally gave us each our own room upstairs, and continued to rent the other two bedrooms. My sister and I both hated this situation, because we were not allowed to use the bathroom upstairs, since that was for the renters. We had to stay in our rooms with the door closed anytime we went upstairs. Our doors had chain locks, which we set every night. We also had to change the beds, dust and vacuum the rooms, and clean the bathroom for the renters every Saturday morning. I was never comfortable with these strange men staying in our house.

Sometimes, the renters would be sitting on the porch when I came home from school. Occasionally, Aunt Lucy would watch football games with the men in the living room and would even pop popcorn to share, while watching T.V. She obviously enjoyed their company. I would go outside or leave the house during those times. This was not normal and felt unnatural. None of my girlfriends lived in this type of home situation and their parents would not allow them to spend the night at my house. I always went to their house for a sleepover.

One night when I was twelve, my sister and I were in the living room, and Aunt Lucy was in her bedroom. One of the men, a new renter who had just moved in, came downstairs and sat on the couch beside me. He said he wanted to show me something and pulled some playing cards out of his pocket. He turned the cards over revealing nude pictures of women. Without warning, he suddenly thrust his hand between my legs and I jumped up in fear and shock. My sister ran to tell our aunt, who made the man leave the house immediately, after filling his ears with some choice words. I was disgusted and afraid, but my aunt did not speak to me. This was the only incident of that nature that occurred during the years I lived with my aunt, but I never forgot it or how it made me feel.

Typically, I rarely watched T.V. with our aunt, except when the Billy Graham crusades were broadcast. She liked to watch his sermons, and I would join her in the living room on those occasions. I was drawn to the power of the words spoken by this man, and I wondered what it would be like to live in a home with a godly father and family. I wanted what he talked about and thought about God during those messages.

When Dad came to Memphis to visit us, we would travel and visit his other family members. A few times, he took us to see our mother in Little Rock for awkward visits. I remember one visit was to a hospital setting and the other times were in different places where she lived, but mother seemed more interested in talking to Dad than to us on those visits. Dad was resistant in response, and those visits were short. A favorite memory on those trips to Arkansas was stopping for ice cream. Dad would always find a local ice cream stand and get us a cone. He had patience with our drips and mess and could make simple things fun. The relationship with his brothers and sisters was altered after the Christmas he left us in Arkansas. They disapproved of our stepmother and did not want Dad to bring her when he visited. Dad took the position that she was his wife and if she was not welcome, then he was not either. That led to very little interaction between them for many years. This was a painful separation as Dad's older brothers and sisters practically raised him upon their mother's death when he was two months old. He had been close to Aunt Lucy through adulthood, and now our stepmother had interrupted his relationship with his siblings. Partly because of the strained relationship with his sister and partly because of my stepmother's interference, we saw Dad only once a year or every other year after that time. Although I felt rejected by him in favor of our stepmother, I was happy when he came for a visit.

Dad called one day to let us know they were coming into town to visit one of our stepmother's sons who was stationed at the Naval Base nearby. On Saturday night, Dad picked us up, and we spent the evening with this young man's family, playing with their kids and bowling. We were still excited when Dad took us back home to our aunt. We ran in the house and shared all the details. She was furious by the time we ran out of breath and threatened to send us back to Texas with our father. She ranted and raved for days and used her words to punish us in response to the evening we had enjoyed with our father. She reminded us of how horrible life had been with Dad and our stepmother and how she was raising us and taking care of us now. In her eyes, we were not supposed to have any loyalty to Dad, and I learned to keep my feelings to myself. Those battles were intense and always ended in a tense silence after a long verbal tirade by our aunt. As we grew older, when my sister and I discussed our childhood, she sided with Aunt Lucy, and I sided with Dad. Our perspectives and opinions always differed.

I walked away from our aunt when she became argumentative, but my sister would stand her ground. They yelled and cursed at each other and even fought physically a few times. I stayed out of their arguments, because I had learned it was a no-win situation. Regardless of how my sister behaved, she was favored by our aunt. Even as young children, her preference for my sister was obvious. My father and other family members were aware of the difference before we were old enough to notice. She looked like my father and his side of the family with the same features and personality traits. I looked like my mother, and with her mental health history, that was enough to condemn me in my aunt's eyes. She was also suspicious, because I was left-handed, clumsy, very shy, and my past history of blackout spells, though these had ceased once I was no longer living with my father and stepmother. I had learned very early that she was not interested in what I was doing at school or in my personal life. She did not attend programs at school that I was involved with, and she only spoke to me with criticism and in comparison to my sister. I felt safer from her scrutiny if I kept a low profile and stayed in the background in her presence. My stepmother had consistently cut my hair very short with sideburns while I lived with her and my father, and I was teased at school by kids who called me a boy. My aunt continued to cut my hair the same way, until I was old enough to insist on letting my hair grow longer.

My sister was beautiful and very popular with many friends. I was quiet and reserved with a small group of close friends. I shut down emotionally at home, but loved school and life outside the house. My sister and I moved in different circles. We were both unhappy and handled life in different ways. She was rebellious and outspoken, while I adapted to whatever was going on around me and absorbed everything internally. We had nothing in common and rarely did anything together. Our aunt had raised us in the same house, but treated us differently. We had no relationship with each other. She would take my sister with her to visit a friend, to shop, or to eat out and leave me at home. Though I did not like being left out, I enjoyed the peace in the house while my aunt was gone. When our Uncle Sam died, Aunt Lucy's older brother who lived in Michigan, she took my sister to the funeral and left me at home alone. The neighbor next door came over and checked on me after school for those few days.

Holidays passed painfully slowly in that house. The first Christmas at our aunt's house was somewhat normal. She had decorated her aluminum tree with red glass balls and plugged in the color wheel, and we had some presents under the tree. We watched the classic Christmas favorites on T.V. She drove us around the city to look at lights and decorations, including a stop by Graceland to see the blue lights lining the winding drive up to the house and the over-sized nativity scene that was displayed every year. My favorite gifts from her that year were a new nightgown and some body powder and cologne. I was delighted to have these personal items. However, the next year, Aunt Lucy said she did not believe in Christmas and was not going to celebrate the season. My sister and I went up to the attic and found the aluminum tree and a smaller artificial green tree with lights and a few decorations. We brought down the small tree and found a box to set it on to add some height, as the tree was only four foot tall. Our aunt said she did not want it downstairs, so we placed it in front of a bedroom window in my room. There were no presents, no lights on the house, no decorations, and no music. The house was dismally quiet and oppressive during the holidays, and I eagerly waited for Christmas break to end, so I could go back to school.

One Christmas, our father planned to spend the holiday with us at our aunt's house. He would come to Memphis, and then we would visit his brother, sister, and their families in Arkansas. Aunt Lucy was going to travel to Texas to attend her husband's family reunion during the same time frame. I was so excited when Dad arrived. He had brought many wrapped presents for my sister and me, and we put those under the little tree in my room. He had faithfully sent money or gifts for the previous holidays, but this Christmas, we would spend time with him and open gifts together. We drove over to our uncle's house in Arkansas, which was about a two-hour drive, the day after Dad arrived. It was a cold, gray day with snow on the ground.

Uncle Lee was about fifteen years older than Dad and a widower. He and Aunt Ola had lived in this house most of their lives, working on their farm and raising a family. It was a modest home off the main highway through town. My favorite part was the metal swing suspended by chains in the screened-in side porch. I liked to sit out there and watch the traffic and the occasional train passing by. A huge garden extended beyond the back yard, which was fun to explore. There was also an old smokehouse on the property, which was kind of spooky, and a mysterious storm cellar with a rusty metal door. One day, my sister and I pestered Uncle Lee about the cellar, until he finally opened it and let us look inside. The steps descended into a round concrete room, and it was very dark and even spookier than the smokehouse. I hoped we would never have to go down in there, as I spotted many spider webs hanging from the ceiling. Aunt Ola and Uncle Lee were the only people I knew who put ice cubes in their milk. She served our milk in heavy glass goblets and I liked drinking out of those glasses. Funny how you remember the small things. Aunt Ola wore an apron, while working in the kitchen. They both had their own chair in the living room situated with a table between them. She would shell peas or peel potatoes in preparation for the next meal, while watching television. We had to be quiet, while the local wrestling program aired, as that was her favorite program to watch on Saturdays. The garage walls were covered with tools and neat rows of old license plates from years past. Uncle Lee would cut off a chaw of tobacco after dinner and tell lots of stories. He had been a square dance caller in his younger years and was a great storyteller. I did not know the people he talked about, but I liked hearing the memories he shared. Usually, our visits in the past had included a ride to the local cemetery where many of our father's relatives were buried. I would look at the tombstones, more names without faces, trying to feel a connection to those family members who had passed on prior to my birth or while I was a young child.

Aunt Ola had died a few years prior to our visit with Dad this Christmas. There was no Christmas tree or decorations, but I was just happy to be with Dad. My sister and I were watching T.V. in the living room, while the men were visiting in the kitchen, when suddenly the phone rang. My stepmother had gotten drunk the night before and was in jail somewhere in Louisiana. Unbelievably, Dad left us there in Arkansas that same day. We had no tree, no presents, no father. My uncle called our aunt in Texas, and she arrived the next day to take us back to Memphis. We celebrated Christmas with some sparklers that Uncle Lee bought at a nearby convenience store.

During the summer when I was twelve, I spent a few weeks with my mother in Little Rock. In my heart, I did not want to go. I had never felt comfortable around my mother the few times I had seen her and had no idea what to do if she got sick. My sister was not made to go, but I had no choice. Mother lived in an efficiency apartment in an older house and worked as a waitress in a Downtown coffee shop. She would go to work very early every morning and leave some change on the dresser for me for spending money. I would entertain myself until later in the afternoon, then walk to where she worked, and we would walk home together. During the days, I walked all over town, browsing in thrift stores, as well as trying on clothes in the stores on Main Street. Sometimes, I stopped at the soda fountain. We also attended a neighborhood Catholic Church and mother provided a small round lace covering for my head when we attended mass. I sat in the pew and watched mother move between the pew and the prayer boards, holding a rosary. I do not remember how we ate meals or where we ate, as mother only had a hot plate on the small kitchen table in her one room apartment.

One day, I saw an ad in the newspaper from a tire store offering a plastic picnic dish set for sale. Mother did not have any dishes, and maybe this set would help. I had enough money saved to buy the set and I spent most of the day walking to the store and back to the apartment before time to meet her at her job. I hoped she would be pleased, but she said nothing when I gave her the dishes, and we did not use them.

While I was staying with mother, my father came through town for a short stop. He was on his way to Memphis to pick up my sister and then was traveling onto Michigan to visit family members. He had stopped to see if I wanted to go as well. My heart was screaming yes, but the look on my mother's face in response to my delight in seeing Dad prompted me to say no. I cried inside when he left. I would have had more fun with Dad, and I wanted to meet his family up North; however, I did not want to hurt mother by leaving early. During my time with mother, we visited the local fairgrounds and played Bingo. One weekend, we rode the bus to a nursing home in Searcy, Arkansas, where my grandmother lived. I had remembered seeing her only once before when I was very young. I do not recall any meaningful conversations with my mother. We did not talk much to each other, but she did talk to other people. She was my mother, but she was a stranger.

Mother wrote to my sister and me through the years that we lived with our aunt, sending cards or letters, and she called us fairly regularly, always on a pay phone. I listened to the familiar sound of coins being deposited by mother before we could talk and then the operator would break in after a bit, prompting mother to deposit more coins for more minutes. When a long stretch of time passed without any phone calls or cards, I knew that she was sick again. Eventually, she would contact us after those lapses in communication, and the return address was always from the same hospital in Arkansas.

The next year when I was thirteen, my sister and I came home from school one Friday afternoon, and mother was sitting in the swing on the porch. I knew immediately that she was not well. She was dressed nicely, but her eyes were vacant and detached and she had lost weight. When she was taking care of herself and staying on her medication, she maintained a healthy weight. At some point, typically, she would stop taking her medication and eating adequately, with a drop in her weight, followed by hospitalization. I never knew what triggered these changes, but I observed them through the few years of her visits.

I was apprehensive as I walked onto the porch. A neighborhood friend crossed the street and yelled a greeting. I quickly walked out to the sidewalk to stop him from coming up to the house, as I did not want to explain about my mother. My sister had gone into the house. She rarely spent any time around mother, and I was left to entertain our mother alone every time she visited. As I walked back onto the porch, mother was distant and not talking. I walked over to the swing where she was sitting, and before I could sit down, she grabbed my arm. Startled, I looked at her in fear. She had never acted like this before, and I was filled with uncertainty. Squeezing my arm, she ordered me to say, "To hell with Jesus." I tried to pull away from her, but she gripped my arm tighter, insisting that I say those words. I did not want to say that about Jesus. My mind was racing. Should I refuse to obey her? I remembered that the Ten Commandments said to obey your parents. Would I go to hell for saying those words? As I was wrestling with those questions, she yelled at me again and tightened her grip to a painful level. Completely frightened now, I quietly repeated the words. I felt sick in my heart. Silently, I immediately started telling God that I did not mean it and had only said the words, so mother would let go of my arm. I wanted to cry. I wanted someone to rescue me. Why was I out here with her alone? Where was my aunt? Why didn't someone interrupt before I had to speak those words? Mother let go of me as soon as I spoke those words, while I was lost in those moments of despair. She stood up and walked past me off the porch without speaking. I followed her, as she walked out to the street. I watched her as she continued moving down the sidewalk, touching every light post and looking up, speaking out loud. I was upset and I was afraid. I ran into the house to find my aunt in her bedroom. I told her that mother was sick and needed help. She just sat there, unconcerned, and I did not know what to do. Somehow, mother made it back home, but much time passed before we heard from her again at the familiar hospital address.

Usually when mother visited, she arrived by bus on Friday night. On Saturday, I would spend the day with her shopping downtown, and she would travel back home on Sunday. We would ride the bus downtown and get off in front of Shainberg's Department Store on Main Street. Mother wore a large shoe, and only the more expensive stores carried the larger shoe sizes at that time. I enjoyed walking into the grand stores that anchored Downtown Memphis. I liked the store displays and the large store windows, and I studied the other people shopping. We would typically have lunch at a coffeehouse on a side street. Our last stop was Lowenstein's Department Store on North Main before riding the bus back to Aunt Lucy's house. Mother would get up the next morning and travel back to Arkansas.

On one of her visits, she brought her youngest son, Davis, who was in his mid-20's. He lived in a rehab center in Little Rock, because he had epilepsy. His mental functional capacity was equivalent to a twelve-year-old. He was happy to meet us, and we played board games for a while and talked and later visited a local mall. It was the first and only time I saw my half-brother. Tragically, just a year or so after that visit, he was killed in an accident. He had left the center where he lived and hitchhiked from Little Rock to Memphis. While walking on the Memphis-Arkansas Bridge on a foggy morning, he was struck by a semi and killed. The truck driver did not see him and was not guilty of any wrongdoing. We did not hear from mother after that time.

I came home from ROTC drill team practice one Saturday afternoon, one month after my 16th birthday, and my aunt told us that one of mother's brothers had called. She was in the hospital and needed to undergo abdominal surgery. If she survived, a second surgery would be required. Mother wanted to see us and the family had called to ask us to come to Little Rock. My aunt planned to get up the next morning and drive us over to the hospital. The phone rang early in the morning. Mother had passed away at 1:45 a.m.

Standing by her casket at the funeral, I thought about what I knew of our mother. She had chosen our names from a baby book and was the only person who called us by our middle names. She always signed her cards and letters with "Love, Mother Helen." I recalled what my father had shared about her behavior before he had her committed to a hospital the first time. They were planning to move, and mother was supposed to be packing one day while Dad was at work. When he came home, she had spent the entire day completely dismantling a brand new sewing machine. Another day when he came home from work, my sister and I were out on the sidewalk by the highway riding tricycles, while mother was unaware that we were not in the house. I remembered climbing up on a cabinet for my mother's purse one time looking for some money. I then took my sister by the hand and walked down the alley to the little neighborhood grocer to see what we could buy with the coins I had found in mother's purse. We walked out the door, while mother was sitting at the kitchen table smoking and talking to the ceiling.

I also remembered walking with mother to a neighborhood Catholic Church. I did not understand the words or the altars, but there was a sense of soothing reverence while in that church. I liked the flickering candles in the red glass candle holders. Mother prayed in front of a statue of the Virgin Mary and dropped coins into the metal box beside the candles. Dad found her outside nude on another day when he came home from work. He became afraid of her after the night he came home carrying a box of toys and some blankets, and she met him at the door with a butcher knife.

Years later, when going through our aunt's boxes of old pictures, we found part of a color photo that had been cut around my father's face. I had asked Dad about it, and he explained that this was part of a large color photo of our family. Mother had cut the picture into little pieces, leaving only his face intact. She had torn all the pages out of the family Bible that my dad had bought as well. Listening to the singers at her funeral, I was relieved that she was not going to be sick anymore and that I would not be burdened with spending time around her in fear again. I would no longer have to lie about her mental illness and face the rejection associated with the truth. I could explain that my mother had died following surgery, and that would end any further questions. I felt guilty that I was relieved. I did not want her to be dead; I just wanted her to be okay and hopefully now, she was at peace.

During the funeral, my aunt's presence was of some comfort with the strange faces staring at my sister and me, comparing us just like my father's family did, and talking about us as though we could not hear their words. An old woman, whom I did not know, asked where our father was and made an ugly remark about him when I did not respond. I moved away from her without speaking. I retreated from mother's family, refusing to acknowledge the brother and wife who had kept us for a short time when we were little girls. I watched dispassionately as they took pictures of mother in the casket and the family groups. There had been no interaction with us or communication from them, until her death. They were all strangers.

What would mother have said to my sister and me in the hospital before her death? Would she have said anything or just looked at us? Would she have touched us? Death is final. There is no chance for change, no time for a new beginning. I had hoped and prayed as a child that somehow my mother would become normal, and I would have a mom like everyone else. She had never been my mom, and now I would never have a mother.

A short while after the burial, Aunt Lucy called to apply for mother's Social Security benefits. She discovered that mother's brother, who was the beneficiary on her life insurance, the same brother we had lived with following our parents' divorce, had informed the court that our mother had no dependent children. Aunt Lucy traveled to Little Rock with the proper documents to file a claim. When the first check arrived, she opened two savings accounts at her bank and divided the check equally, with each half deposited into separate accounts for my sister and me. She was very upset with mother's family and angry that they had lied about the existence of her youngest children.

Many years passed before I returned to the cemetery in Arkansas where mother was buried, which was more than one hundred miles away from where I lived. Time had distorted my childhood memory of the drive to the cemetery. After a day of fruitless searching, my husband and I stopped at the funeral home in Newport for information. We discovered the cemetery was actually about twelve miles from town. Following the directions provided, we drove out of town and turned onto a secondary highway that was vaguely familiar, following a river with long S curves. Although I did not recognize the cemetery entrance, I did remember that she was buried under a large tree on a small rise where the gravel road curved around, situated towards the rear of the cemetery. I was surprised to see that Davis was buried next to her, and irises had been planted on mother's grave. The familiar questions replayed without answers, as I stood there looking at the headstone, all that remained of mother's life. Eventually, I tracked down her sister and her oldest brother, asking for information or any pictures of her they would share. No one had been willing to help my father when mother became ill, and perhaps now, they would help shed some light on her past.

The yellow brick house felt familiar, as I walked up the steps. I knew I had been there as a child. This was mother's only sister, many years her elder. She had no pictures, but she told me that when mother was a teenager, she would disappear for a weekend and then come back home like nothing had ever happened. She said they did not know where mother went or what she did while she was missing. I later found an older brother who lived in Illinois, and we communicated by letter a few times. He was in his late 80's and sent a few photos with his letters. I had written asking for information about mother and her illness, but he never answered any of those questions. Instead, he told me about his children and grandchildren. He passed away about a year later, leaving me with the familiar list of unresolved questions.

All I knew about mother was what my father and his family had shared. They could not answer questions about her childhood or first marriage. My mother and her first husband had two sons. Her oldest son, Djuanell, had joined the military as a young man and started his own life. My father did not have any other information about this son. For years, I burned with unanswered questions about her and her past. Dreadful fear that I would develop the same illness plagued me into middle age. I wondered if I would know if I was losing my mind. Would everyone around me see changes, while I remained unaware? How would I know if I was changing? Would any future children inherit this illness? My sister and I only agreed about two things while growing up--we shared the same fears about our mother, and we did not understand why we had been born.

Both parents were married previously, and both had two children from their first marriages. Mother was in her 30's and Dad was in his 40's when we were born. My mother was the 11th child in her family, and my father was the youngest of ten children. His mother died at age thirty-eight when he was two months old, and only five of his older brothers and sisters survived to adulthood. There was a large gap between the older and younger siblings. Both of my parents had lost a child from their first marriage. Mother lost Davis in an accident, and my father lost his oldest daughter, Caryl, to illness at age twenty-nine. My sister and I attended Caryl's funeral as young children, and it was the first time I remembered seeing my father cry. We were not connected to these other siblings, and our aunts, uncles, and cousins were all much older. Our grandparents were dead before we were born, except one grandmother who died when we were children. We were so far down in birth order that we never felt like part of the family. Though I enjoyed being around our aunts and uncles and hearing their stories, I felt far removed from their lives. They were all in their 60's and 70's, and we had shared no history with any of them.

Chapter Eleven

Young Love

I was not allowed to date until I turned sixteen, and I had started exchanging messages with a boy at school at age fifteen. He rode his bicycle beside me, while I walked home from school every day. His school day ended an hour earlier than mine, so he would go home, get his bike, and come back to school to walk me home. He found my phone number in ROTC class and called me that afternoon. My aunt's rule was five minutes max on a phone call, and I warned him about the time limit. When our call ended, he waited about fifteen minutes and then phoned again. My aunt answered the phone. She called him everything but his name and hung up before he could respond. Undaunted, he called back the next night and every night after that, keeping within the five minute time frame. We started dating after my birthday and continued to date off and on through the 10th and 11th grades. I fell in love with him, as much as you can at that age. He gave me a lot of attention and wanted to be with me all the time. He showed me more attention than I had received at home or in my family. Teenage emotions are intense, and I was devastated when he broke up with me on my next birthday. I felt everything deeply and was hurt by his uneven behavior. He began a cycle of breaking up and getting back together without reason or explanation. During a long spell when we were not together, I met the cousin of a girlfriend's boyfriend. There was some physical attraction, but I did not know him very well. We saw each other a few times on double dates. While we were parked one evening, I gave up my virginity. I was aware of a voice saying, "No, No, No," but the other voice reminded me of those same thoughts that had continued since early childhood: It does not matter what I do, because no one loves me and I am just another throwaway kid who will not amount to anything. Who cared if I was a virgin? I was not precious to anyone. Girls like me would not meet Prince Charming and wear a beautiful wedding gown. I did not have the right kind of parents or family. Weddings like that were only in the movies and fairy tales.

Soon after that night, I discovered I was pregnant. I was consumed with fear. Fear of my aunt's reaction scared me more than the reality of my situation. It had been a battle living with her the past few years, and this would definitely knock me out of the house with no place to go. My father and stepmother would never accept a pregnant teenage unwed daughter into their home. All of the fears about my mother's illness contributed heavily to my rejection of this baby. I knew enough about the streets to admit that I could not survive homeless and I did not want to try. A friend at school told me about a physician who performed abortions in his home, and I called to schedule an appointment. I never heard from the father of the baby again. The boyfriend I had dated off and on came back into my life at this point. He offered to marry me and raise the child as his own, but I quickly dismissed that idea. We were too young and had no means to raise a child, as we were still in high school. I also did not believe he would accept the baby.

I made up my mind to abort. I went to the bank and drew out enough money to cover the cost from my savings account. My boyfriend picked me up early that Saturday morning and took me to breakfast. We then went to the doctor's office, and I learned I should not have eaten any-thing that morning. I felt nothing as I sat in the waiting room and nothing during the procedure. I threw up repeatedly afterwards. My boyfriend stayed with me, until I was able to ride home and the nausea and vomiting had subsided. I was numb inside and out, mortified and ashamed at what had just happened. I stayed in bed at home the remainder of the weekend and returned to school on Monday morning. From that point forward, I blocked my feelings about the abortion and did not allow myself to feel anything connected with the baby. Looking at myself, I believed that it would be better for the child to be in heaven, rather than unloved or uncared for on earth.

During my junior high school years, I had wondered about my future. I wanted to go to school after graduation and see what I could become in life. Maybe my tomorrows would be better than my yesterdays. I had no definite plan or idea how to make it happen and no one to help guide or counsel me on reaching any future goals. My aunt's only advice concerning my future was, "Why don't you marry that ol' long-haired boy you've been dating?"

My boyfriend and I continued our relationship. We had exchanged hundreds of notes during our time in high school, sharing our expressions of love for one another. One Saturday morning, we went to a local state park with another couple for the day. My aunt had told me to be home at two o'clock in the afternoon, which would only allow four hours, and the trip to the park one way was about an hour. I always came home on time and my sister never did, and suffered very little for her disobedience. I decided to stay out until 6:30 that evening, risking a probable grounding and another tirade from my aunt. However, I was not prepared for her reaction. She was waiting on the porch, and as soon as I got out of the car, she started yelling and calling me every name that popped into her head--whore, tramp, slut. These were the same names she had called me when I was still a virgin, after seeing me holding hands with a neighbor boy when I was fifteen. I had been so mortified by her behavior that I never spoke to that boy again.

My aunt was out of control this time, and I was embarrassed and afraid. My boyfriend got out of the car and crossed the yard. Taking me by the arm, he directed me back to the car and said he was not going to leave me with her. He took me home with him, and I did not return to my aunt's house. His parents allowed me to spend one night and then told their son I could not stay with them. He decided we would move out and live on our own. He worked in a local grocery store, and I worked part-time for the summer at the school board. We went to the city clerk's office for a marriage license, because I was going to need permission from the court due to my age. My aunt was only a custodian, and guardianship was required to grant permission for marriage. We spent most of the day at court and obtained the court's approval. We were married in June of 1976 in the church parlor where he had attended church as a child, with his mother and sister in attendance. We rented our first apartment using his older brother's identification.

I had shared with the women at work about my marriage and our desire to return to high school together. They kindly gave us some wedding gifts and explained that school policy did not allow married students to attend the same school. We appealed to the proper department at the school board, and during a subsequent meeting, it was explained to us thoroughly about our expected behavior and strict guidelines to follow. We would be allowed to attend our same school as a trial, but at any time, that decision could be rescinded if our behavior was found to be inappropriate.

Chapter Twelve

HAPPILY EVER AFTER

We went back to school for our senior year, and I quickly realized that it was going to be very difficult to do this without support. My friends stopped talking to me, and I had no one to interact with at school except my husband. His friends were more accepting towards him about our situation, but I was completely ostracized at school. We struggled to keep up our studies, plus jobs, and adjustment to married life as two teenagers. I had been placed in a part-time position in a medical office following my summer job, and life was now more about rent, food, and utilities. At the end of the first semester, we decided to drop out of school. I was emotionally a wreck. Nothing in my life was the way I wanted it to be. The only thing that had ever made me feel proud was my work in school, and now it was ending in shame and humiliation. We were required to take a sheet around to each teacher from our classes and have them sign off on our exit from school. Silently, as I went from room to room, I was hoping someone would say something personal to me to encourage me not to drop out, to stay in school, to help me figure out a solution. Apparently, I had not made an impression on any of my teachers, as they all signed the paper and handed it back in silence. All except my homeroom teacher--she wanted me to return my Honor Society certificate and said she was going to have that stricken off my record. She was angry and ashamed that I was in an organization where she served as a sponsor. I had been inducted during the 10th grade. I could not wait to get out of the building. I was disappointed in myself, my family, and the school. No one had any expectations for my life. I was nobody.

Shortly after our wedding, I broke out with some type of infection that was so painful I could hardly walk. My husband took me to the doctor. While I do not remember the clinical diagnosis, I will never forget the treatment. My genital area was swabbed with some type of liquid medication that was dark purple. I was then placed under a heat lamp completely exposed for the time required for the medication to dry. Humiliation washed over me every time I visited the doctor, and several treatments were required for complete healing. I felt dirty and shameful. I believed I was being punished for the abortion.

Surprisingly, our marriage bloomed. We passed the GED exam after dropping out of school and matured somewhat after two years of learning to live together. My husband had found a much better job with benefits and a very good salary. He was responsible, dependable, and ambitious, and I was proud of his accomplishments. During the years of his employment with that particular company, he was offered the opportunity to go back to school to earn several certifications and licenses appropriate for his job. He was favored and promoted.

I started working as a medical transcriptionist at a major hospital in 1979 with good pay and benefits, and we were established financially. We bought our first house within a few years, and in 1981 our first child was born. Our son was the first grandchild and first great-grandchild in the family, and he brought so much joy into our lives. The same fears about my mother's mental health increased during my pregnancy, but I did not talk about those and just prayed all would be well. Five years later, our daughter was born. I had a husband, a home and children--my own family, people to love who loved me in return. For the first time in my life, I felt connected and normal as a wife and mother. We celebrated every holiday and birthday. We took vacations and weekend trips with our children, and we enjoyed our free time as a family.

My children grew up hearing childhood stories about their father and other members of his family. His family was a part of our holiday celebrations and birthdays. The lack of representation from my family was painful. There were no stories about me as a child growing up, or birthday or Christmas memories to share. My greatest joy in my marriage came from my children. I loved being a kid with them through their childhood and watching them grow and learn. As they played, I was thankful for the privilege of being a mother to my son and daughter. Life and marriage had started out rocky, but I was now content.

My children's extended family was comprised of my husband's family. Every holiday season, I would invite Aunt Lucy over for a visit in hopes of having some family representation. My husband's family routinely asked if I had seen or heard from my aunt, and I would give the expected negative response. One year, close to Christmas Eve, she dropped by with my sister for a quick hello, tossing an unwrapped packaged tablecloth onto the dining room table. She stayed about fifteen minutes and then left. Her visit was more painful than if she had not come. The tablecloth was never used, and I stopped inviting her after that year.

My father had been involved in our lives throughout our marriage. We had visited Dad and vice-versa on a fairly regular basis, until my stepmother's death in the early 1990's. My life started falling apart soon after, and Dad was lost in his own grief. My children were not old enough to have an established relationship with him at the time of his death in 1997.

I had tried to witness to my father as a teenager. Following my salvation and baptism at age twelve, I began worrying about my father, fearing he would go to hell when he died. I wrote him a long letter explaining salvation the best way I could and waited excitedly for his response. I was crushed when he wrote back sternly dismissing my message. I continued to pray for my father for decades. He was not interested in God during my young adult years and frequently used God's name as an adjective for the weather, the traffic, or any irritants in his life. He could be very rigid at times, in a hurry to get somewhere and then in a hurry to return home. Dad reached out to his brother and sister in Arkansas following my stepmother's death, and they reconnected after all those lost years. Uncle Lee and Aunt Ora passed a short time later, and I was very thankful that they had not died without speaking. My father started going to church during his grief, and I was very surprised when he shared that with me on the phone. He said he told the preacher that he had a lot of questions, and I assured Dad that he was in the place for answers. I encouraged him not to be embarrassed, as we all continue to learn until we move to heaven. My last conversation with Dad was on my birthday in October of 1997. I had moved into the safer location, I had my truck and a good job, and I felt optimistic about my future. Dad expressed his concern for my situation, and I reassured him that I was doing much better and life was somewhat easier. I did not want him to worry, as he had suffered a major heart attack a few years previously. Believing my struggles would cause him undue stress, I had not shared all the details of my circumstances. He had been somewhat incredulous when he celebrated his 80th birthday just two months prior, sharing his surprise that he had lived that long. He said he did not want to be the last one to die in his family, but he was the youngest sibling and Aunt Lucy had died in 1996, leaving him the only surviving child from that generation. The following Sunday afternoon, the phone rang. My father had passed away earlier that morning from congestive heart failure.

I was completely devastated. At the time of my marriage at age seventeen, my father and I were not maintaining contact. The loss of communication with my dad hurt my heart, and during my early 20's, I decided I wanted a relationship with someone in my family. The only choices were Aunt Lucy or my father. I would have to accept my stepmother in order to see Dad. I would make that concession, because I knew that I would never be close to my aunt. One day, I picked up the phone and called Dad. Several years had passed since we had last spoken, and I was not sure how he would respond. Relief mixed with assurance filled my heart when he answered the phone. He was very happy to hear my voice, and in that moment, I understood that Dad was thankful I had made contact, because he did not know how to make the first step. I was glad that I had made the call and removed that barrier. We talked at length and made plans for a visit. As the conversation drew to a close, I found the courage to tell Dad that I loved him. To my great delight, he responded, "I love you, too." I did not remember hearing my father say that when I was a young child, but from that point on, every time we spoke on the phone or at the end of a visit, we always hugged and told each other, "I love you."

I did not know my father as well as I would have liked. Short visits did not allow for insightful conversations, but sometimes, I would get a glimpse that revealed a little more of this man I called Dad. During a visit when my son was about three years old, I watched Dad interact with him in sweet surprise. He was at ease and patient with his grandson.

I smiled as I watched Dad toss a tennis ball into the air over and over, while encouraging his grandson to try to catch the ball as it rolled off the roof. I remembered watching my father feed him a bottle as an infant and then several years later also playing with my baby daughter. Her first pictures were taken wearing a dress Dad had sent through the mail following her birth. Precious memories. Born in 1917, my father's childhood was filled with poverty and hard work. Love was not spoken or given in his home. He worked in the fields all day for very little money, and his father had charged him room and board as a young teen. He had left home at age fifteen.

God blessed me once again, as I did not have the funds to travel for Dad's funeral. My best friend at work asked our employer and coworkers if they would donate money for gas and a hotel room, instead of sending flowers. They presented me with an envelope of money the day before my trip, and I was overwhelmed once again by the kindness of other people. I wanted my children to go with me, but their father told them they did not need to go, because they were not close to their grandfather. I was terribly hurt by his attitude, as he had no concern for my feelings. Emotionally, I could not make that trip alone, more than 1000 miles round-trip, and I insisted to Joe that he ride with me instead. I did the driving, crying off and on during the day. We arrived safely in Beaumont that evening, though emotionally distressed. We found a hotel room, ate a quick dinner, and by then, exhaustion had settled in.

The next morning, we went to the funeral home, and Joe stayed in the vehicle, while I went inside. I was informed that Dad's body had already been loaded into the hearse for transport to the cemetery. I broke down in tears and explained that I had driven over 500 miles. Seeing my distress, a member of the funeral home staff kindly offered a private viewing. He set up the casket in a viewing room and left me in silence. As I looked at my father, I was overwhelmed by loss. Dad was the only family member I felt connected to, and we had not been as close as I had wanted. My children were not with me, and I felt completely alone. Typically, I found comments distasteful about the appearance of the dead in the casket; however, I found myself assessing my father's face and was pleased to see that he looked peaceful.

I thanked the funeral home staff for their compassion, and when I walked outside the building, I threw up multiple times. Dad was gone and I would never see him again. Life had become one nightmare after another, and I was desperately trying to maintain composure, as I drove to the cemetery. I was happy to see my half-brother, Jay, from Michigan there as well and I sat next to him, crying throughout the graveside service. The minister from Dad's church said our father hoped that his children would learn from his mistakes. I was thankful for her reassuring words that God had heard my prayers about my father throughout the years. The only peace I had was the knowledge that Dad was in heaven.

Chapter Thirteen

DIVISION

My husband was the dominant personality in our relationship, and I had felt smothered by his control and manipulating selfishness. During the early years of our marriage, and even after our son was born, he was jealous and possessive. I was faithful to my husband and valued our marriage vows. I was home with him when I was not at work, and he knew where I was at all times. He would become upset if I was five minutes late getting home from work. He did not want me to leave the house while he was at work, even if I was with his family. This controlling behavior continued, until a breaking point one Saturday morning when our son was about 2-1/2 years old, after visiting a trendy hair salon to get my first perm. This salon was highly recommended by a coworker and I drove to the salon in excited anticipation. The stylist cut and shaped my hair, and I felt beautiful when I walked out the door. I drove home excited about my new look, but when my husband saw me; he became upset and tried to force me into the shower to wash the perm out of my hair.

I moved back into my aunt's house with my son for almost eight months. This was a miserable time for my son and me, and deep down, I knew I would eventually have to go back to his father. I had married him and we started a family, and I was going to stay married for my son's sake. When I moved back into our house, surprisingly, my husband had changed, perhaps matured, because the unwarranted jealousy and possessiveness had disappeared. He was calm and more settled, though the sarcastic criticism continued.

We both wanted a second child, a younger sibling for our son, and we were blessed with a daughter five years following his birth. Soon after her arrival, my husband started talking about a vasectomy. I was crushed by his lack of desire for more children. He felt that we had one of each and that was enough. I had wanted perhaps one or maybe two more, but he insisted that he did not want additional children. I persuaded him to wait, until our daughter was one year old before proceeding. My heart was heavy while I was sitting in the waiting room almost thirteen months later, and I shed some tears during his procedure.

My husband became critical of my appearance, while our daughter was a young child. I was a size 18 three years after she was born. One morning in 1989, while I was getting ready for work, he told me I really needed to do something about myself. I was crushed and hurt tremendously by his words. He was fond of making sarcastic remarks that cut and then laughing afterwards, an ineffective attempt to soften the hurt. I was very sensitive to his criticism, and his verbal jabs and remarks always pierced. He seemed unaware, and each time I confronted him, he would say I was overreacting.

The hospital where I worked was participating in a liquid diet program through a university. Hospital employees could enroll at a discount. I wanted to please my husband with my appearance, and after talking to him about the program, I enrolled. I ate no solid food for three months. The liquid diet provided all the required nutrients and satisfied the appetite. I could only have water or other liquids without additives in addition to this diet. I dropped about forty-five pounds and lost four pant sizes during that time. I worked out every workday at the hospital's fitness center, which accelerated the weight loss. I was thrilled with the results and expected my husband to be excited as well. I was looking forward to wearing more attractive clothing and for my husband to be proud to have me by his side. Unbelievably, even after this sacrifice and profound weight loss, he looked at me the same way, and nothing changed in our marriage.

He then began to criticize my job, because he felt my salary was not adequate for our lifestyle. He said I needed to go to school and improve myself. My employment as a medical transcriptionist was not glamorous, but it provided steady income. I became weary of his constant criticism and withdrew further emotionally. This affected our sex life as well. I did not withhold or barter sex, but I could not respond in the way he desired or deserved. I wanted to have a healthy sex life with my husband, but his years of sarcasm and criticism had affected my confidence and my level of desire, and I was not able to share myself with him physically in a mutually satisfying manner. I felt inadequate sexually during our marriage, and he even accused me of being frigid. I was a failure in his eyes in every area of our marriage.

My husband had worked swing shifts and weekends at different times throughout the years. Whatever his job required, we adjusted the family routines according to each shift change. We were now working opposite shifts, and I would leave for work, as he was coming home from his job. One morning in June of 1995, while I was dressing for work, my husband asked me to sit down, as he wanted to talk. I sighed inwardly, preparing for the occasional budget lecture. He proceeded to tell me that he was not happy and was going to file for divorce. He was tired of the responsibility of being a husband and a father. He had been married to me for half of his life, and he wanted to see what else was out there. He had already talked to his mother and was going to move back to her house. When I came home from work later in the evening, he had removed all of his clothing and personal belongings. We had been married seventeen years. I thought we would be married until death, that we would watch our children grow up and marry and start their own families; that we would be grandparents, and then pass on at a ripe old age. I had not planned for divorce.

We had entered Chapter 13 bankruptcy for reorganization of debt several months prior to his leaving and in five years, we would be debt free. When we initially started the plan, all of the garnishment came from his check, but he had recently requested that I share in the garnishment, so that his paycheck would not be so diminished. I agreed, though reluctantly. He worked for a large company that was familiar with these types of legalities. However, I worked in a small office and would have to share my personal business with the administrator, so he would be prepared when the paperwork arrived. I was making about $12 an hour, and the garnishment was a heavy burden. We had no savings, as I had used my annuity from my previous employer in the purchase of our home a few years prior. My immediate primary concern was having enough money to pay the bills and provide food for my children. Our house note was far above what I could pay on my salary. I sold some antiques and furniture for immediate needs, and then I sold my wedding set and other jewelry. The utilities were cut off at one point. The house was nearing foreclosure when my husband's sister, who was a realtor, found a buyer for the house. Initial relief was replaced by panic when she added that the buyer brought a full price offer, but wanted possession of the house in ten days. Two of my coworkers helped me pack. Another coworker had a friend who managed property rentals. After several desperate phone calls, the property manager agreed to accept me as a renter, but I would have to pay first and last months' rent, plus deposit. When the house closed, I cleared $2000, just enough to pay the required rent, and utility and phone deposits. I had lost my entire annuity, all that I had saved from my years of employment. Life had fallen apart. I had lost my husband and my identity. I had no purpose, no hope. What kind of future would I have now?

In September of 1990, I was diagnosed with salmonella. We were out of town for the weekend when I became ill. I did not see a doctor, until we returned home and by the time the diagnosis was confirmed, it was too late for treatment. The illness rode its course, until the symptoms stopped. In January of 1991, I experienced the first of many attacks that I thought were due to the salmonella. The episodes came on suddenly, without warning, with concomitant vomiting and diarrhea, followed immediately by itching and swelling of my hands, accelerated heart rate, profuse sweating and heat throughout my body, with redness of my face, upper chest, and legs. My heart would race so fast that I felt like I was going to pass out. I would lie on the floor in between the surges of these symptoms, which repeated every few minutes, until the vomiting and diarrhea subsided, usually two to three hours in duration. These spells were severe in intensity and very debilitating when they occurred. The episodes were followed by extreme fatigue and weakness that typically lasted through the next day. I saw a GI consultant and he performed some tests, without a definitive diagnosis established, and I assumed it was some type of residual from the salmonella.

One day in September of 1993, I was at work when I experienced a sudden onset of wheezing and difficulty breathing that progressed throughout the day. I called my physician's office and was worked in to see the doctor that afternoon. The wheezing was so pronounced that she decided to send me to the ER for further evaluation. She said she could send me home with several inhalers, but she felt I would end up in the ER later in the evening, so it was better to go straight to the hospital now. My admission diagnosis was "asthma attack." Per protocol, I was taken for a ventilation/perfusion lung scan, which was expectedly negative. During the test, I was required to lie flat on the table, and by the end of the study I was lightheaded and my breathing had become shallower. After the test, I was resting in my room looking out the window at the night sky when a technician came in with STAT orders to draw arterial blood gases. It seemed only a few minutes had passed when a nurse came into my room and said my oxygen level was 51% and they were giving me a high dose solu-medrol IV slow push right away. Breathing treatments were started at regular intervals as well. I remember asking myself, "Am I really that ill?" I was weak, unable to take a deep breath, and dizzy. I had no idea what was really going on in my body, but I did not feel "right". Breathing treatments and steroids were continued the next day. On the third day, when I was to be discharged, I developed a butterfly rash on my face and a rash on my legs. I was diagnosed with a systemic disorder and referred to a rheumatologist upon discharge. I had suffered a similar episode in 1992 with a sudden onset of wheezing and difficulty breathing, at which time; I was diagnosed with acute bronchitis and placed on an antibiotic and several inhalers.

I visited the rheumatologist following my hospitalization in 1993. After a lengthy consultation and review of my records, he diagnosed systemic lupus erythematosus (SLE). I was skeptical that I had any disease and did not completely accept that diagnosis. Even though at that time, I met more than half of the criteria for SLE, it did not seem possible that I could have a chronic illness. I was placed on Plaquenil, a prescription medication, for several years without any complications, and those horrendous attacks that had persisted following the salmonella diagnosis ceased completely.

During these times of illness, my husband became increasingly irritated and critical. The fatigue and weakness were becoming more of a problem, and he resented the changes in our home life. He grew impatient with my inability to keep up with him and the children at times. I continued to work full time, but came home from work exhausted and without any energy. I was concerned about myself, as I did not understand this change in my body. I felt guilty that I was unable to manage everything at home. I believe my husband's fear of my future health and its effect on his lifestyle contributed to his unfaithfulness and subsequent departure from our marriage.

We lived in a suburb of Memphis, and I had a forty-five minute commute to and from work. My husband took his truck when he moved out, and I drove the Grand Marquis that had belonged to his grandmother. Though the car was a smooth ride, it guzzled gas, and every extra dollar I could earn was required to maintain the vehicle. With all the disruption in their lives, I wanted to keep my children in their same schools. The move had changed their assigned school district, and I wrote a letter to the school board explaining the circumstances to request permission for them to attend the same schools. Permission was granted with the understanding that I would have to provide transportation to and from school, as they were not on the bus route.

I was filled with despair every time I looked at my children. I was consumed with fear about the future and how we were going to make it financially. I only made enough money to last one week, and my next payday was another week away. I worked overtime as much as I could, and then started working another part-time job just to make enough money for food and basic needs. Several times, I wrote a bad check with cash back for gas. I knew by the time the check ran through the bank again, my direct deposit would cover the amount and any fees. I continued this pattern until one day when I went into the bank to make a deposit and was informed my account had been closed. I had been turned over for collection for the bank fees from all those transactions. I appealed to my sister and her husband for the money to hire a lawyer to file for chapter 7 bankruptcy, so that I could get back on my feet. They agreed to send a check to the attorney for his fees.

My husband moved out in June of 1995 and was going to file for divorce soon after; however, he delayed filing, until it was beneficial for him financially. He had earned his real estate license and worked for a realty company, in addition to his regular job. I had taken on extra work at home aside from my full-time job to help cover those expenses, as well as an appropriate wardrobe. We filed income tax for that year as married filing separately. I was due to receive a large refund and was anticipating getting bills paid and having some money in the bank. Instead of a check, I received a letter informing me that my total refund had been applied to the tax bill due for that year. My husband's real estate commissions had affected our income and since we were both married, though living separately, I was jointly responsible for the tax burden. Now I understood why he had not filed for divorce sooner. He phoned me to let me know he would pay the balance due of a few hundred dollars. I was sick, disgusted, and angry. I did not deserve this. He was the one who had abandoned the family and, as I discovered later, had been unfaithful during our marriage, but I was the one who was losing everything. His life was not affected adversely. His family helped him get back on his feet quickly, and he was soon able to buy a house in the same neighborhood where his mother lived.

Chapter Fourteen

DEFEAT

Even though I could not afford the rent for the house I had moved into after my husband left, it was the only place I could find. Because of the chapter 13 bankruptcy, the property management companies would not consider me for a rental. After a few months in the house, I fell two months behind on the rent, and another month was almost due. With the help of Joe, a man I had met at an auction, I negotiated for a special sale to sell all my extra furniture, household goods, and miscellaneous items to try to make enough money for the overdue rent. Amazingly, I made just enough to pay the three months' rent. My closest coworkers traveled out to the auction site and bought a few items in support as well. I watched as possessions accumulated during my marriage moved across the tables and out the door. The years represented in those items disappeared with nothing left, except scars and memories.

I had two girlfriends at work who cried with me, sharing hugs and words of encouragement and prayers. Occasionally, they slipped some money in my purse or bought lunch on hungry days. I prayed without faith in my prayers, as I did not believe God would help me or that He cared about my situation. I was unloved, unwanted, and abandoned all over again.

The first weekend after my husband moved, his sister and her husband invited me to go with them to a local auction, so I would not be sitting at home alone. Surprisingly, I really enjoyed the evening. My mind was distracted from my problems at home, as I studied the people around me and watched the flow of selling and buying throughout the evening. The building was old, with peeling paint on the ceiling and a dirty concrete floor. Rows of tables filled one side of the room, and furniture for the sale was arranged on the other side with chairs in the middle for the bidders. Reality faded for a few hours every Saturday night. My son had no interest in the auction and stayed home, so I took my daughter with me for a few weeks. I had no money to entertain my children on the weekend, and this was someplace to go that was free. I rarely bought anything other than food at the snack bar.

My children spent a lot of time alone at home due to my work schedule and the auction on Saturday nights. I was outraged when their father called one night and said that I needed to stay home with the children, instead of going to an auction. I reminded him that the children would not be alone if he had not left the family. He also forbade me from using his family as a babysitter on the auction night, stating he would take the kids to visit his family when they were with him. Anger and rebellion raged inside at his continued control and manipulation.

The kids were not happy living with me. We had no extra money, and life was unpredictable and boring. There was no security living with me. They were at home after school alone, until I got home from work later in the evening and part of the weekend when I attended an auction. I had no family to help and they missed their extended family. Their father no longer allowed me to interact with his family, and my children only saw their other relatives when they were with their dad. Their father had been repairing the house he had bought in his mother's neighborhood and was almost ready to move. My children each had their own bedroom and had chosen their room colors and accessories. He walked me through the house, which was on the same street where their grandmother lived. He proposed letting the kids live with him, so that they would be close to his family after school and would not be alone as often. His house was not far from where I worked and it would be convenient to drop by and pick them up. I talked about the situation alone with my children. My son, who was fourteen, told me that he loved me, but that he wanted to live with his dad. My daughter, who was nine, had always been a daddy's girl, and she cried for her father. She wanted to live with her brother and her daddy. There seemed to be no end to the losses in my life.

I was not able to hire a lawyer for the divorce or the amendments to our original agreement that my ex-husband had petitioned through the court. Now, I wanted representation for this next step. I used my bill money to cover the fee for my own attorney. My heart was heavy, as I headed to the courthouse that afternoon. I sat alone on a bench in the hallway outside the courtroom, while my children's father and his girlfriend were sitting down the hallway talking and laughing with his lawyer. I later learned that this was the same attorney she had used in her divorce. She had wrecked her family first, and then my husband had left his family. Now, they were here together with her lawyer. I was filled with shame, hate, and anger, and I felt outnumbered. My husband had left me, and my children did not want to live with me. Rejection rushed over me in waves.

My lawyer appeared and joined their lawyer in close conversation. He finally approached me and explained the situation. My son at age fourteen would be allowed to tell the judge where he wanted to live. My younger daughter would be taken into the judge's chambers for his decision. He showed me a chart for the State of Tennessee and the child support percentages for two children. My financial obligation would be almost $600 per month; however, the lawyer for my children's father was willing to accept $350 a month, if we settled out of court. Stunned, I listened in utter disbelief, as my lawyer explained that I had missed a court hearing, and this information was going to be used against me. He also informed me that every time I had left the children, my daughter had reported that to her father, per his instruction, and the lawyer would present a record of the dates and times. In addition, the one incidence when I had been reported to child services by their father would be presented in court as well. This single incident was a case of my bad judgment. My son was going to a movie with a neighbor's family one Friday afternoon and would return home to be with his sister. I was going to the auction that night and left before he came home, with the understanding that her brother would be home in thirty minutes; however, unbeknownst to me, the neighbor had decided to see a different movie, which started later in the evening, and my son was late getting home. Scared, my daughter had called her father, because she was alone and did not know when we would be home. He phoned the sheriff's office and filed a complaint against me, and I was ordered to visit Child Services in response. I had met with a counselor downtown and explained the situation. I was filled with shame, embarrassment, and remorse for my unwise decision and for my daughter's fear in being left alone. The counselor explained there was no specific legal age when a child could be left home alone, and this was assessed according to the maturity of the child. She advised that my daughter, at age nine, was not old enough to be left alone based on her reaction to this one instance, and I assured her this would not happen again. No further action was required. I was relieved when I left the building and angry that her father had filed a complaint against me unnecessarily.

I had no more money to give my lawyer for additional legal fees to fight and all the odds were in their father's favor. I did not want my children to have to make a decision in court who they wanted to live with, as I was concerned how it would affect them emotionally in choosing one parent over another. Their father apparently did not have any such concerns in his pursuit of custody and child support. My lawyer advised me to accept the reduced child support, because if I went before the judge, I would be ordered to pay the full amount. I felt like a fly in the spider's web, trapped without any chance of escape, as I glanced down the hallway in defeat. The victors were already celebrating. I had nothing. Everything I cared about was gone.

I was almost running when I left the courthouse. I was losing my mind in the panic that was consuming me. How had my life reached this point? I had done nothing wrong. Everything was going his way, while I was falling apart. I drove home in tears. I had no one to call, no one to talk to. I looked at my bills and my checkbook. There was no way I could pay out an additional $350 every month. My husband earned almost twice my salary, and his girlfriend was a pharmacist and also drew child support. Why was I ordered to pay child support? Where was justice?

The office administrator where I worked was a Christian, and he was very concerned about my situation. When my house sold, he rented a large moving truck and brought several employees from the office to help me move into the house I would be renting for the next year. He had been understanding and accommodating with my schedule changes due to school hours and personal issues. He informed me that my payroll records had been subpoenaed and that he had been ordered to appear in court as well after failure to appear in a previously ordered hearing. He had spent a considerable amount of time on the phone and discovered that a court order addressed to me had been sent to an old address from about five years ago. The order for his appearance had been sent to a satellite office address, rather than the main office where I was employed. The administrator was on vacation when the original office order arrived and was not in town for the court hearing. I had never received notice of that previous court hearing. He addressed a letter of explanation to the court and an appeal on my behalf. I could not believe the depth of deceit the father of my children had sunk to in desperation for control and money, plus his lawyer had used unethical tactics to win a court battle. On top of everything else, I was ordered to pay the attorney fees for his lawyer. I had no idea who the man had become that I had been married to for almost two decades.

Just two weeks later, my ex-husband called me at work on a Monday morning. He had married his girlfriend over the weekend and was planning to move out of state as soon as the school year ended. I broke down at that point. My friends helped me to the bathroom. Through convulsive sobs, I shared what had happened. They were stunned and angry, with many choice words voiced by my friends. Exhaustion set in once I calmed down. I was sinking under defeat upon defeat upon defeat.

My children denied any prior knowledge of their father's plans. They had wanted to live with him in his house on the same street as their grandmother, so they would be close to me and their other family members in Memphis. They did not know he was going to get married that weekend. He and his girlfriend had sprung it on them as a surprise shortly before the ceremony. I called my former mother-in-law, and she also denied knowing in advance. Indeed, he had plotted his course well in advance of leaving our home.

As Spring approached, I had to think about my financial situation. The children would be leaving at the end of the school year. There was no need to stay in a three bedroom home that I could not afford with the added child support burden. I moved into a low income apartment in West Memphis, Arkansas, just across the Mississippi River from Memphis, for $325 a month. Two sisters lived next door advised me not to move anything valuable into the apartment during the daytime. They warned me that thieves kicked in the doors without knocking. I used the back door when I left the apartment and kept a very low profile. A coworker and her sister drove over from Memphis and helped me move some large items one night into the apartment. As they were carrying the mirror that attached to the dresser, the mirror suddenly fell through the backing and shattered all over the sidewalk. Dismayed, I tried not to dwell on the old superstition of seven years of bad luck.

Six weeks later, I received a call from the resident manager. She explained that she managed another complex for the same company that was located in a safer area. She told me I did not belong in this neighborhood and was going to let me move to the other complex without any additional charges. The manager also said she would transfer my deposit. I packed up and moved again, grateful to leave that neighborhood behind, and thankful for this unexpected blessing. I felt somewhat settled and secure in the new location.

My children had left town, and I had not heard from them since their move. I could not afford phone, cable, or internet, so I was not able to talk to them, except while at work. I did not trust their father and did not want to see him or hear his voice. I would not tell him where I lived. I was barely functioning with the loss of my children and the devastation of lack, only going to work and back home at this point. My friends at work were worried about me, as I moved through the day on auto-pilot. I had nothing and had been discarded and thrown to the curb. My children's father had married the woman with whom he had been unfaithful during our marriage and moved my children into her house. She had built a new home and relocated prior to their marriage. My kids were with him, and I had to pay him child support, until they reached age eighteen. I lived in a low income apartment and paid out every dollar earned for child support and living expenses. My food staples consisted of peanut butter, bread, cereal, and milk. I moved through the days constantly fighting despair. My mind was a battlefield of hopelessness and unworthiness. Sometimes, a voice would tell me to give up, that life held nothing for me, and that I had no future, but something inside pushed me to hold on, to survive. I fought to continue, to stay sane, and to believe in hope.

My car had become a major issue. With close to 100,000 miles, something constantly needed repair or replacement. I had no extra money and would not travel out of town, because of fear of a break-down. In the event of problems on the road, I had no cell phone and no one to call. The transmission had started slipping recently. I came out of the grocery store one day and the car would not move. I had it towed to a local transmission repair shop, and the cost was going to be substantial. I had called my father at that point in hopes that he could help, as I had no other option. I had never asked my father for any money and did not know how he would respond. To my delight, he was very concerned and sent me a check for more than I had asked. The shop kept my car for almost two weeks. I lived a great distance from my job, and there was no bus route. I did not know what to do, as I would lose my job if I could not work during the time frame of the transmission repair. One of my coworkers kindly offered to pick me up every morning and drive me home every afternoon. This was a tremendous sacrifice for her, as we lived about thirty miles apart, not including the added distance to the office. She faithfully carried me to and from work every day and offered to take me anywhere I needed to go. I could not repay her for her kindness, and I asked God to bless her and her husband abundantly for their support.

This same girlfriend was also concerned about my inability to travel to see my children. She contacted a close friend whose brother worked at a car dealership and asked him to find a good used vehicle with low mileage and a reasonable car payment. Within two weeks, I was driving a like-new 1995 Ford Ranger pickup with only 13,000 miles and a note I could manage. I had not driven a standard shift in many years, but it all came back to me when I sat in the driver's seat. I felt an incredible sense of freedom and safety as I drove it off the lot that day. I turned the radio up loud and headed out to the interstate thanking God for this tremendous gift and blessing for those who had helped in this deal. The first thing I did was call my kids and schedule a visit for the next weekend. Four months had passed since I last saw them and I was thrilled to be able to see them again in a roadworthy vehicle. Their father had offered to bring them to town to see me, but I had refused. I was still very angry with him and did not trust him and would not tell him where I lived.

To celebrate this change, I started ballroom dancing lessons through a local college off campus. I found a class where a partner was not required and went every week. My heart felt lighter than it had in many, many months. I still had the same problems, but a seed of possibility had sprouted.

Close to the time I bought the truck, I received a phone call from a previous coworker, whom I had worked with in 1990 to 1991, with a job offer. Two years prior, she had called about a job opportunity, but I turned her down, because of the unpleasant family situations I had remembered previously in that office. When she called this time in 1997, she assured me those situations had been resolved. I listened to the details of the job and asked about the salary. She said she would tell the employer that I was interested, and he would call me directly about the wage the next day. I was wondering how much he would be willing to pay and how much I should request. That evening at home, I received a call from the woman who currently held the position for which I was being considered. Surprisingly, I had worked with this woman at the hospital back in the 1980's for a few years. She had heard of my life circumstances and that I was being considered for her job. She explained the job in more detail and told me what salary to request, assuring me I would get that amount. My mouth hung open in amazement, as this would be a $2.25/hour raise from my present job. When I talked to the employer the next day, he agreed to my salary request. I was going to be able to breathe once again; I could manage my bills and have a little bit of margin. Gratitude overflowed, as I thanked God for His blessings.

The loss of my children left a huge void in my life and my heart. I kept myself busy to escape the emptiness and to temporarily stop the endless replay of my thoughts. When I was not working, I attended auctions and later helped Joe at a flea market. I continued to attend the same auction on Saturday nights and eventually started going to another auction on Friday nights. I met Joe at the Saturday night auction where he worked the tables.

Chapter Fifteen

JOE

Within a couple of years after my children moved away, I was back on my feet financially. I had spent every other weekend with them, and I also drove over after work through the week on the occasions when my daughter was performing in the school band. I talked to my son and my daughter about living with me, but they wanted me to leave things alone and not make any changes. I was emotionally devastated, as it had been my driving hope during the past two years to be a part of my children's daily lives once again. I wrestled with this decision and my motive. What was best for the children? More disruption in their lives and school changes now that they were established? I thought about the upheaval of moving so many times and changing schools I had experienced as a child and how that had affected me. I wanted to protect my children from that pain and any emotional punishment they would suffer from their father and his family. The old familiar rejection washed over me anew, as the realization sunk in that the living situation with my children was not going to change. The years without them were lost forever and nothing would bring those back.

In 1999, I had a dream, which was just a single image. I saw myself in my truck driving down the highway pulling a trailer. I knew when I woke up that I was to move to the same city where my children lived. Inspired and energized, I updated my resume and composed a cover letter to send to the larger medical practices in that city. I faxed the resume and letter to multiple offices. Two days later, I received a phone call in response and scheduled an interview for the following week. I was filled with renewed purpose in my life for the first time since my children had moved away.

The office where the interview was scheduled was about seventy miles from where I lived, and I left home that day with time to spare for the drive. It was a very hot day in July with a heat index of 100+. I was halfway there, driving through a small community on a secondary highway, when I had a flat. Unbelievably, a state highway truck in front of me noticed I was pulling over onto the shoulder and he pulled over at the same time, stopping in front of my vehicle. The lone driver approached and said, "Looks like you need help" and walked past me on the shoulder. As I voiced a relieved response, he removed the spare and the jack as though he knew exactly where they were located and quickly changed the tire without any conversation. I tried to thank him, but he waved it off, as he walked back to his truck and drove off.

Incredibly, I arrived at the office only five minutes late. The interview was favorable, and the office environment was pleasant. The salary was a concern, as I would have to take a deep cut of four dollars an hour from my present pay rate. I worked in a large city in a competitive medical field, and this smaller city had no competition in the region, setting their own market scale much lower. I wrestled with the loss of income in my mind. I felt reassurance in my spirit to accept the job, and I did, but with reservations about how this salary cut would affect my life.

I visited this city again over the next two weekends in search of a place to live. The first weekend, I spent the day looking at different apartment complexes with my daughter and applied for the one we liked best. My application was denied after a credit check, and I returned the next weekend to search again. I found an ad posted in the newspaper for a newly constructed duplex, very reasonable, with utilities and cable included. After viewing the property and meeting with the owner, I signed a lease and paid the required deposit. Everything was settled, and now I needed to pack and move once again. The same voice that had urged me to take this job did not tell me to take Joe, who was now living with me following the death of his mother. The idea of leaving him behind made me feel uncomfortable. How could I put him out? What would happen to him? I battled with this until the last minute when I decided to take him with me, though I knew I was supposed to go alone, and just hoped it would all work out somehow.

I needed money fairly quickly to pay for the expenses involved with the move. Unable to qualify for a loan due to my bankruptcy, I talked to Joe about possibly having an auction to sell the vintage items I had saved from my divorce. He was in favor of the idea as he also had some merchandise he wanted to sell, and he negotiated the details with the auctioneer and his wife. Joe would work the table, as we would be the exclusive sellers, and we agreed to pay the auctioneer and his wife a flat rate for their services. We set up the sale for a Saturday night and spent that day unpacking and displaying all the items, filling most of the tables. Dealers arrived from the surrounding areas, many who had traveled some distance, and the room was full of people before the sale started. I had prayed and asked God to provide the money I needed for all the expenses with the planned move, and I felt hopeful as I scanned the crowd. The sale far exceeded my expectations. Indeed, all of the regulars were shocked at how well every item sold. Everything brought a better price than I had hoped, and my spirits soared, as the evening progressed. The auctioneer and his wife were also amazed at how high the winning bids reached. Joe claimed credit for the night's success with his skills, but I knew God had blessed this auction. He had provided more than enough money to cover the expenses of relocating.

Not surprisingly, because our event was so successful the auctioneer decided to host another special sale, but Joe and I were not allowed to participate. This sale would be only for specific dealers, as well as the auctioneer and his wife. Joe wanted to attend the sale, as he was always looking for a deal, plus we were both curious to see if the auction would be as successful. The tables had all been covered in white tablecloths, and everyone participating was dressed nicer than usual. Anticipation was high as the sale started, but quickly turned to stunned disbelief, as the bids were very low with some items bringing no bid. The auction ended early with very few sales. I was even more in awe of God's abundant blessing of provision for the upcoming move.

My new job was easier and less stressful than my previous employment, but I continued to worry about my income. The woman who was hired to replace me at my previous job had not been able to keep up with the workload, and I had been asked to continue working on the weekends to help manage the volume. This provided extra money, but was also a long commute. One Friday afternoon, about six weeks after starting her employment, this woman walked out of the office and did not return. When I heard what had happened, I jumped at the opportunity to return to my previous employment in Memphis and gave notice on my new job. I did not believe God would provide for all my needs as punishment, because I had not obeyed Him about Joe. I had been able to spend more time with my children, but my relationship with Joe had deteriorated greatly to the point that we could not continue living together. We were no longer involved with the auctions or the flea market, as we had moved away from that environment, and Joe had become negative and resentful about his situation in life. He had made decisions long before I met him that had affected his current position, and I did not accept any responsibility for that; however, I did feel guilty once again for getting involved with this man and allowing him to become dependent upon me. He was living with his mother when I met him, and they had their own daily routine. She was a kind woman with simple needs. She loved her son dearly and said he was the only person who could make her laugh. I felt uneasy that I had interrupted their lives, but she once shared with me that having me around took some of the pressure off of her, and she asked me to stay with her son. I did not understand her words at that time, but I was reminded of them upon her sudden and unexpected death soon after that conversation. Joe was lost without her, and I had taken him under my wing partly to fill the void in my heart from the loss of my children. Now, almost two years later, I readily admitted my mistake. My guilt over this relationship had convinced me that God was angry with me for my disobedience, and I moved on without seeking His guidance. I could not put Joe out on the curb, though he was making no effort to help himself. I decided to move back where I lived previously to be closer to my job and also to motivate Joe to relocate.

Joe was born in Memphis to an Italian father and a Mississippi mother and was raised Catholic. His grandfather had arrived from Sicily many years previously. He grew up more Italian than Mississippi, peddling fruits and vegetables with his brother as a very young boy for his father who owned a neighborhood store. Selling came naturally to Joe, but not his younger brother. Joe sold extra to cover his brother's shortage. Joe was a high school football star, and his father reveled in his attention in the local newspaper and the neighborhood, winning Joe favor for his athletic success. He learned at a young age how to use his natural charm.

I met him in the late 1990's. Most people either loved him or hated him, but everyone knew who he was. Even if they disagreed with him, people liked to hear what he had to say. He loved to laugh and make others laugh, and he had an endless supply of stories. We were not romantically involved and did not have a physical relationship, but I felt drawn to him, in spite of this lack of physical connection. He kept details about his personal life on a "need-to-know basis only." However, over time, he shared some of his story with me. He joined the Army after college and was stationed in California. He remained on the West Coast after discharge, married and had a child, divorcing after several years. He later married his second wife and lived a very different lifestyle. He suffered a stroke in his late forties and eventually returned to Memphis. His mother said he came home a different man, broken after losing everything he valued. During his life in California, he had made choices that his family did not approve of. That division never healed. His mother told me that before attending family events, she would make Joe place his hand on the Bible and swear not to cause any trouble. Apparently, these family gatherings would start out pleasant, but would eventually spotlight on the differences between Joe and his brother and the choices Joe had made in his life. Joe never backed down from a discussion, an argument, or a fight. He would get beat up walking to school as a kid, but he stood his ground and fought his battles. He was charismatic, very intelligent, and his eyes never missed anything going on around him. He could take it all in and respond without blinking. However, he never conquered the condemnation from his family.

His relationship with his daughter was a casualty of those choices. Joe would occasionally babysit his grandson on the weekend, so that his daughter and her husband could travel to dog shows, as they were breeders. Sometimes, I helped him at the flea market, and other times, I took his mother to the beauty shop or the grocery store.

Joe became ill many months later, and I took him to an internist I had worked for in the past. After a physical examination and discussion, the doctor advised me to enroll him in the VA, as Joe was a veteran, for medical care, as he was going to need extensive testing and evaluation. I helped him enroll and then took him to the Social Security office to see if he would qualify for any benefits. He was entitled to receive a check every month that was not a great sum, but enough to sustain him. Once these programs were started, friends from the auction circle helped him get settled into an independent living facility funded by Catholic charities. This transition took time and required a lot of patience. He did not go happily into this change, and a mutual friend from our flea market circle took charge of him during that adjustment. When the holidays came around, I invited Joe for Thanksgiving and Christmas dinner. My children continued to spend those days with their father and his family, as they had since childhood, and I knew Joe would be alone on those days as well. I continued to visit him every week or so to share a meal and talk. He did well, until the next summer when he started experiencing severe abdominal pain, but repeatedly refused to go to the doctor. We had been through an extensive ordeal the previous summer when he was hospitalized three times in two months with a kidney stone that was too large for lithotripsy, eventually requiring surgery and multiple follow-up visits. He had told me he would never go back into the hospital again.

One day our mutual friend called me at work to tell me that Joe was severely ill. He had gone over to check on him and had to ask the resident manager to let him in, as Joe did not answer the door. Apparently, he had been in bed a few days, with nothing to eat or drink. Our friend stayed with him several hours and tried to get Joe to go to the hospital, but he adamantly refused. I went over as soon as I got off work. When I saw Joe lying in his bed, I was shocked. He did not seem to be aware of my presence. I sat on the bed beside him and told him I was there. He never looked at me. His gaze was fixed on a corner across the room at the ceiling, and his eyes were glazed. In a voice barely above a whisper, he asked me to sit with him and hold his hand. After sitting with him for awhile, I decided I had to do something. I could not just sit there and let him die in that dirty bed. I called an ambulance and had him taken to the hospital. He was admitted to the ICU.

I later learned from our friend that Joe's daughter and son-in-law had come earlier to his apartment and had removed the remainder of his flea market inventory, his food, his personal items, and his truck. The son-in-law had held Joe's hand while he signed the title to his truck and his Social Security check, and then they had walked out leaving Joe in the bed.

During the three previous hospitalizations, his daughter had only visited Joe once for a short period of time; however, I had continued to keep her informed of his progress. When I called her the next morning to tell her that her father was in the hospital, she became very angry. Her voice rose as she was speaking, to the point of yelling, and she said, "He is going to die sometime, and you have to let him go." The hate in her voice through the phone gave me a sick feeling deep down inside. She was practically screaming at me that her father had never done anything for her; he was never there for her when she was growing up, and she did not owe him anything. Stunned, I asked her, "How long are you going to hold onto that hate? Are you going to take it to your grave?" She hung up. I tried calling her again, but she would not answer the phone and would not return any messages. The hospital called her repeatedly, as she was the only person who could legally make decisions regarding her father, but she did not answer those calls and did not return any of their messages. We never spoke again.

The first night in the hospital Joe looked better and talked normally. His only request was that I would not let him be embarrassed, and I reassured him I would take care of everything at his apartment. The second night was unpleasant. He was angry, talking wildly and saying hurtful things to me. He was looking at me while he spoke and appeared to be in his right mind, as he suggested that I should commit suicide. I had never seen him in this condition. One of his doctors pulled me out of the room and explained that they had given him medication and not to take anything that he said personal. The third night the curtain was pulled around his bed and the lights were off in his room. One of the doctors I had seen previously was standing at the nurse's station and saw me approaching. We talked about Joe, and then she put her arm around me and said, "Iris, I want you to go home and do not come back. Just remember him as you knew him." I found my way to a private waiting room and sat there in numb silence for a long time. Thankfully, no one was in the room, and I remained there undisturbed as I cried and prayed, trying to accept that Joe was dying. My dream in 2000 about Joe came to mind with the realization this was now being fulfilled. The dream was more of a picture, a snapshot of a single image, rather than a series of events. I could still see it clearly in my mind:

I was standing on a platform outside of a house trailer, and there was water all around the platform. The bank of the Mississippi River on the Arkansas side floods every Spring, and the high water forces the people who have campers and trailers along Dacus Lake, off of the river, to move their vehicles up to the access road close to the interstate. This floodwater was where the trailer in my dream was situated. I had never lived there, but it was a familiar scene, as I traveled through this area every day back and forth across the bridge to Memphis to work. Stranded on the platform, I watched helplessly as Joe moved away from me and out of reach. His upper body was positioned in the open mouth of an alligator. The lower body of the alligator was hidden below the dark murky water. Joe had one arm raised, seemingly asking for help, though I could not hear any words, and I was powerless to offer any assistance. The alligator was not thrashing or biting; he was just holding Joe with his mouth wide open, slowly moving away from the trailer. When I woke up, I knew Joe was going to die. I had thought it would happen soon after the dream, but two years had passed since then, and the dream had moved to the back of my mind.

A few days later after the hospital visit, I received a call from his cousin that Joe had passed away over the weekend, early Saturday morning, in August of 2002. She was one of the few people in his family who truly loved Joe. I had listened to them sharing stories from their younger years, and the mutual affection had been obvious. I called the morgue to make arrangements to bring over his suit and clothing for burial. I was informed that as soon as the daughter signed the release papers, he would be buried in a local military cemetery. The morgue would call me when it was time to bring over his clothing. I spoke to the woman at the morgue several times over the next few days. I was dismayed at the delay. The morgue repeatedly tried to reach Joe's daughter to finalize the paperwork for burial, but she never returned the messages and did not go to the hospital. His nephews then arranged for his body to be moved to a private funeral home. The viewing and service were for "family only," and an obituary was not published. His daughter did not attend the funeral.

My children and I made sure that Joe would not be embarrassed. We disposed of the soiled bedding and the mattresses. We carried the few remaining furnishings out to the curb, cleaned his apartment, and donated his clothing.

Joe received Last Rites. He had read the Bible many times and had studied different religions throughout his life. He shared with me that the Monsignor had encouraged him to enter the priesthood as a young man, because he was so inquisitive and questioning, but Joe had not been interested. He had been blessed with many gifts, abilities, and talents. How would his life have played out had he chosen a different path? I hoped that he had made peace with God before he left this earth.

He went to his grave under the condemnation and judgment of his daughter, and most of his family. No last words, no forgiveness, and upon his death, his body lay unclaimed in the morgue for five days. Many times, I have wondered what his daughter did with all that hate, withholding love and forgiveness, once she could no longer punish Joe. I have prayed over the years for his daughter for a relationship with God, as He is the only one who can help her forgive her father and heal her heart and give her peace with the past.

Chapter Sixteen

BROKEN

Joe came into my life when I was very vulnerable emotionally. I gave him too much of my time and attention that was inappropriate for our casual relationship, trying to fill the emptiness in my life without my children. My faith was weak, and talks with God infrequent. I did not understand my own behavior, and I did not trust God in my decisions. Revelation and healing came through much prayer and spending time alone with Him. Eventually, I was able to forgive myself, as well as Joe. He had been aware of my emotional vulnerability and had used it to his advantage during our time together. I had hurt my children, not intentionally, but damage had followed the brokenness.

Weekend visits with my children were typically uneventful. My son started working part-time and on weekends when he turned sixteen, and his visits became less frequent. Saturdays were spent at the Laundromat, and T.V. provided entertainment later in the evening. Sunday came quickly, and my heart was heavy during the drive back to their father's house. Sometimes, if my son was home, we would share a meal at a local fast food restaurant. Driving home alone was always tearful and filled with prayer and conversation with God. Life was empty without my children. I missed the nightly hugs and the "I love you's" we had exchanged in earlier years as a family. Now, I only received a hug every other weekend. I did not know how to adapt from taking care of my children daily to a mother on alternate weekends only. Every goodbye felt like a punch to my broken heart. In their father's eyes, my role seemingly was to pay child support and provide babysitting. He had altered the weekends; so that my children were visiting me the same weekend their stepmother's children were with their father, in order for them to have a weekend to themselves every other week. I resented his control and manipulation of everything concerning the kids through those years, but I held my tongue out of love for them, as they did not want me to make waves. At times, there was a raging battle inside me between peace and rebellion in dealing with those issues.

One day, while I was still driving the old Grand Marquis, their father called and said the kids wanted to meet me on Sunday morning. I could pick them up at his mother's house and take them for breakfast and bring them back. While we were on the phone, I agreed to come, but after we finished speaking, I felt that old spirit of rebellion and resistance rising up in my heart. No one ever told me that my children loved me or missed me. At her father's prompting, my daughter called if I was late with the child support check, to remind me that it was the law that I had to pay her daddy. Anger and resentment mounted, as I focused on my own pain. My role with my children had been reduced to working and sending money to their father, enabling him to do everything with them that I could not afford. I was not a part of their daily lives and would never have the opportunity to experience all the moments I had missed. By Sunday morning, those old thoughts had replayed so many times that I was convinced my children were not interested in seeing me.

I was helping Joe at the flea market when my kids and their father came into the building. I saw the pain flash across my son's face in the instant before he turned around and walked out. My daughter was crying so hard she was sobbing and could not talk. Immediate conviction struck me full force. My heart broke for their pain and mine. I held onto my daughter and cried with her. I told her over and over that I loved her and that I was happy to see her while holding onto her. Shame washed over me at my attitude. I had hurt my children in response to the anger and resentment towards their father. He explained that they had been so upset when I did not show up earlier that morning that he had to bring them over to see me. I did not trust him, and part of me believed that he had done this intentionally in spite of the pain it would cause the children. My son did not want to talk to me that day. This was the only instance I had failed to meet them at an appointed time, and I had hurt them unnecessarily. In my reaction to their father in anger, they had received the brunt of that misguided blow. I prayed many times for God to forgive me for hurting them that day, to help my children forgive me, and to help me forgive their father.

Children traditionally lived with their mother after a divorce. As a young idealistic woman, I was critical of mothers without their children, assuming they were morally corrupt, alcoholic and/or addicted to drugs, or mentally ill. Now, I was in that situation, but I did not fit into my own narrow condemning categories. I worried what people would think when they discovered that my children lived with their father, and that fear and shame kept me trapped in social isolation for years. It was safer to keep to myself than to open up to more rejection. The little voice was always ready to remind me of my failures and my past, assuring me that people would shun me if they knew the truth.

During the years following their father's remarriage, I would not speak against him to my children. He was their father, and they needed to respect and obey him, regardless of his choices. I forced myself to keep my opinions and negative comments to myself and reminded them that their father loved them, in spite of what had happened to our marriage. It was very difficult to be fair to him, but deep down, I knew it was the right thing to do and best for my children. My son had felt betrayed by his father. He had agreed to live with his dad, because they would live in Memphis in close proximity to their grandmother and continue in the same schools. When his father surprisingly remarried and announced they were moving to another city, my son felt betrayed. My daughter, as she grew older, also saw the truth.

My only connection to life was my children, and I had missed precious moments of their daily lives. Many special occasions had been celebrated without my presence. I had continued to allow them to spend every Thanksgiving and Christmas Day with their father and his extended family, as had been the custom when we were married, and I would see them a few days after the holiday. Most holiday seasons were spent alone, and I learned to accept the solitude of those days, trying to dwell on the blessings in my life rather than the losses. I decorated a Christmas tree every year with our family ornaments and set out the children's past annual pictures with Santa. I mentally relived happier days and thanked God for my children and for the sweet memories. There were lots of tears and my heart remained heavy. I had cross-stitched Christmas stockings for my children when they were young and those were dear to me, because each stitch reminded me of the work involved and memories from past holiday seasons. The first Christmas after their dad and stepmother married, he called me and asked if I would let the kids have their stockings. He explained that he had tried to buy new ones, but they insisted on having those I had made when they were younger. After much conversation, I finally relented and gave the stockings to my children.

During the years my children lived with their father and stepmother, I was not allowed to park in the driveway or walk up on the porch. When I picked up the children, I had to wait in my vehicle outside at the curb, until they came out of the house. Their father refused to communicate with me directly about these types of issues and repeatedly used the children to send messages. I parked out front and waited, as they had requested, and did not complain, choosing instead to enjoy the time I had with them without talking about their father or their stepmother. One evening, my daughter invited me to come to her school and watch her during flag dance practice, so we could spend some time together afterwards. There was a small crowd in the gym, and I sat alone on the bottom bleacher watching her on the floor. Her father and stepmother were seated some distance away, talking and laughing with the other parents and interacting with the other girls, reminding me once again of my isolation and disconnection from their daily lives.

When my son graduated from high school, I attended the ceremony and even sat with his father's family. His father and stepmother hosted an open house for him afterwards, but I was not invited. I cried all the way home from the rejection and pain. I attended my daughter's graduation five years later, and by that time, her father and stepmother had divorced. She chose to celebrate with her friends.

After my children grew older, I talked to them several times one-on-one and with both together, openly and honestly. I apologized to my son and daughter for hurting them. I asked forgiveness for behaving in any way that would cause them to think I did not love them. I told them they were my family and that I loved them with all my heart, more than anyone else, and always would. My daughter, though I saw her every other week, admitted that she had actually hated me for about eight years through some of her teen years and early 20's. She said part of the reason she was able to forgive me was because I never went away and I kept coming back. Their father had provided the stability and security that I could not provide on my own. I resented and regretted that I could not do the same. They had chosen to live with their father, because they believed he could provide a more secure environment. I had to accept that I could not compete with their father or his provision, and I reminded myself that my financial shortcomings did not define me as their mother. Several years after the divorce, my ex-husband made the comment that he had done me a favor when he left, as I had become much stronger over the years and everything had worked out for the best. I felt a sickening thud in my spirit, as I listened to his casual dismissal of my pain and suffering. He had no idea of the depth of the hurt he had inflicted without apology. I cried out to God silently, once again, to help me forgive this man.

I had wanted my children to have a happy childhood and a stable foundation for their adult lives. Their father boasted that he had raised our children, as though I had played no role in their lives, and at times, I was pushed completely out of the picture. I witnessed his selfishness through his controlling manipulation and demand for money and lost all respect for him as a man, as he turned into a total stranger. I tolerated his behavior as well as I could during his second marriage, in order to protect my children from the same kind of emotional pressure I had endured from my aunt and my father. I thought it would help them and protect them if I absorbed the backlash. I was a failure in my expectations to be the mother to my children that I never had as a child.

My children remained in my daily prayers through the years. I prayed for God to bless and protect them, to guide them in their decisions, and to bring them into relationship with Him. I had never prayed as hard for anyone or any situation, as I prayed for my children. Guilt surfaced repeatedly that I had not taught them about Jesus and provided spiritual teaching and connection through church. When my son passed through a phase of rebellion, without damage, my prayers became more fervent. When my daughter was involved in a potentially fatal car crash and stepped out of the vehicle unharmed, I praised God every day for her life. My constant prayer was for salvation, forgiveness, and healing in their hearts and minds.

I had purpose and identity during the years of my marriage to my children's father, and life made sense. When everything fell apart, suffering one loss after another, I thought I would lose my mind. A part of me died through the following years, as I struggled to find a normal state of being amidst the instability of my circumstances. I busied myself with a man who had no respect or love for me, I gave my time and energy to activities that served no lasting purpose, and I struggled financially for years. The child support obligation ended in 2004. Joe had suggested that I drop out of the system and not pay any money, but I had immediately rejected his words. I chose to pay the support and continue my relationship with my children the best I could. When I mailed the last payment, I thought life would improve without that financial burden, but the emptiness, guilt, shame, regret, and remorse remained and continued to hold me with the same distorted perspective of myself and my life. I had accepted every negative generality tossed in my direction from childhood as part of my identity.

God had tried to restore my life and bless me when He gave me the dream to move in 1999, just a few years after the divorce. Everything had worked in my favor with the ease in securing a new job and a nice place to live, with the auction covering all the moving expenses. I had brought Joe with me against God's instruction and subsequently lost my way through fear, doubt, and self-condemnation. I moved back to the same complex where I had lived previously and returned to my previous job, undoing the blessings God had provided, and life continued, uneventfully, until 2005, almost five years later.

Through those years, God repeatedly tried to get my attention for more than a quick prayer, an occasional Bible verse, or a visit to a local church, but I could not accept that He truly cared. I had prayed for large needs and thanked Him when He helped me, but did not know how to relate to Him in all things. I prayed for other people and thanked God when He answered those requests, believing He would help others before He considered my prayers. I was the outcast, the odd one, the one overlooked and ignored. The old lies had continued to play in my mind. I had grown up hearing adults say, "God helps those who help themselves" and believed God's approval and love had to be earned. I had been taught if you do all the right things, then God will reward you with blessings and love. I believed I would never earn anything from God, but judgment and punishment.

During the time I was commuting a long distance to work, I listened to a Christian radio station every morning. There was a stirring in my soul for God, and I struggled to understand Him and His Word. I wanted a relationship with Him, but did not feel worthy, because of the many mistakes, poor choices, and wrong decisions in my struggle to survive through the losses in my life.

After Scott moved to heaven, I reached out to some of the ministry programs I was listening to on Christian radio in Goshen. I wrote a letter to a few of those ministries and received kind letters in response. Most helpful were the CD teachings I received from "In Touch Ministries" titled, "The God of All Comfort" and "The Believer's Valley Experiences." I listened to those over and over through the following months. I began to learn about the nature and character of God through Dr. Charles Stanley's teachings on radio and television. I wanted to know who God was and to know Him on a personal level. I wanted to know who I was and where I belonged. Nothing in my life had answered those questions. Psalm 139 was a familiar passage, but one night, the words became alive and personal, speaking to me intimately.

"1 You have searched me, Lord,
   and you know me.
2 You know when I sit and when I rise;
   you perceive my thoughts from afar.
3 You discern my going out and my lying down;
   you are familiar with all my ways.
4 Before a word is on my tongue
   you, Lord, know it completely.
5 You hem me in behind and before,
   and you lay your hand upon me.
6 Such knowledge is too wonderful for me,
   too lofty for me to attain.
7 Where can I go from your Spirit?
   Where can I flee from your presence?
8 If I go up to the heavens, you are there;
   if I make my bed in the depths, you are there.
9 If I rise on the wings of the dawn,
   if I settle on the far side of the sea,
10 even there your hand will guide me,

your right hand will hold me fast.

11 If I say, "Surely the darkness will hide me
   and the light become night around me,"

12 even the darkness will not be dark to you;
   the night will shine like the day,
   for darkness is as light to you.

13 For you created my inmost being;
   you knit me together in my mother's womb.

14 I praise you because I am fearfully and wonderfully made;
   your works are wonderful,
   I know that full well.

15 My frame was not hidden from you
   when I was made in the secret place,
   when I was woven together in the depths of the earth.

16 Your eyes saw my unformed body;
   all the days ordained for me were written in your book
   before one of them came to be.

17 How precious to me are your thoughts, God!
   How vast is the sum of them!

18 Were I to count them,
   they would outnumber the grains of sand—
   when I awake, I am still with you.

19 If only you, God, would slay the wicked!
   Away from me, you who are bloodthirsty!

20 They speak of you with evil intent;
   your adversaries misuse your name.

21 Do I not hate those who hate you, Lord,
   and abhor those who are in rebellion against you?

22 I have nothing but hatred for them;
   I count them my enemies.

23 Search me, God, and know my heart;
    test me and know my anxious thoughts.
24 See if there is any offensive way in me,
    and lead me in the way everlasting." - Psalm 139 (NIV)

God had created me with my own personality and gifts and abilities, apart from my family. I was not a mistake and my life had merit. The people and events in my life had affected me, but did not define this woman God had created. The rejection and abandonment I had suffered as a child and later in adulthood did not come from God and did not reflect His view of me. I had despised my own weakness and my failure at pivotal moments to do the right thing, and I had walked in guilt, shame, and condemnation for decades. Every wrong decision just added another layer to the already heavy burden I was carrying unnecessarily. God showed me that He loved me more than anyone on earth ever could. Circumstances in my life were not a gauge of His love for me. He had been waiting on me all these years to turn to Him completely and to accept His love. He had purpose and fulfillment for my life, and He would help me to discover more about myself and Him, as I continued on my journey.

I related to the story of Cinderella in my youth and saw myself as that unwanted stepchild in the corner, who only heard her name when there was an instruction or a criticism thrown in her direction, hearing more than once that I was hard to love. Scott was my Prince Charming, whose arrival in my life was unexpected and beyond my wildest dreams. God provided Scott instructions and guidance in his approach to captivate me completely. He enabled me to trust Scott and to receive and share that love. God poured His love into both of us through one another and gave us the love we had been searching for in our lives. I was honored to be Scott's wife the last years of his life and thanked God for that privilege. I have thought about our love and marriage from Scott's perspective. Rereading the words he shared from his heart while we were together reminded me of the depth of his love. I continue to pray for God to bless Scott's soul for loving me so beautifully and completely.

I have lived most of my life trying to fit in, wanting to be normal and accepted, wishing to be loved, and through the love and loss of Scott, I have found everything I searched for in Jesus. Every time Scott wrapped his arms around me, I felt a sense of belonging that I had never experienced. Through my grief and healing, God has replaced all of my emptiness with the knowledge and assurance that I belong to Him and He will never let me go. At times, during my marriage to Scott, I would look at myself in the mirror and wonder what he saw when he looked at me. Now, I smile at myself in the mirror and declare with confidence, "God loves me!" with a heart full of gratitude and joy, excited for what lies ahead. I would not be the woman I am today without the steps I have traveled, and I embrace all the experiences that have shaped my life.

God pursued me relentlessly through the decades despite my resistance, fear, and rebellion, and despite my misperception of Him. Instead of a judgmental God, as I understood in childhood, I discovered a loving God, full of mercy and compassion who desires a personal relationship with all of His children. I thought I would spend all of my tomorrows with Scott, and finding God in the midst of the shock of losing that future has been life changing. God took my broken heart that was chained in bondage to shame, guilt, anger, and insecurity and began to heal the brokenness. He revealed the chains that I was unaware were holding me down, showering me with grace and love, and He set me free. My heart, my mind, and my desires have changed in the process.

The pleasures I once pursued no longer hold any appeal, and the things I once thought I needed have fallen by the wayside. Life has begun again in an unfamiliar stage of bloom.

Chapter Seventeen

BEYOND GOSHEN

My time in Goshen has drawn to a close, and I will leave Indiana in the morning a different woman from my arrival here almost five years ago. I left everything familiar behind when I moved here in 2008 and discovered the source of all love through Jesus. I am ready to move forward, secure in God's love for me and His constant presence.

My desire is to follow God, to listen to His voice only, and to grow closer to Him in my daily life. Life on earth cannot provide the security that I have in Him, and He is the only anchor I need. I remain in awe of the grace He has showered over me, while patiently bringing me into an intimate relationship with Him. Nothing compares to the love of God. I now know, without any doubt, that God loves me and will never leave me nor forsake me. He is with me every breath, every step, and He will continue to direct me along my path under His guidance, protection, and provision. I have the assurance that I will live forever with God in eternity. My circumstances on earth can change in an instant, but God's Word will stand forever, and I rest in His promises. No one and no circumstance can take that away from me.

All of the amazing movements of God in my life have served to re-mind me of His power and strength and ultimate victory, regardless of what I face.

I continue to walk down this road, not knowing where He'll lead me, hand in hand with God. My prayer is that my journey, my life, has in some way inspired, encouraged or equipped you to embrace each and every aspect of your life; each intricate piece of your puzzle, no matter how hard, difficult or unbearable it may have been. Our lives are a part of God's ultimate plan, and many times, we will not understand how or why things happen, but rest assured; God will weave them into a perfect quilt that will reveal His hand of glory upon us the entire time.

I pray that our Father showers you with His grace, as He did for me, and that you can now move forward in the next season of your life with courage, boldness, strength and purpose to fulfill His perfect will for you. There is purpose for everything under the sun. I encourage you to find the light in your situation, no matter how dark it may seem. He is always with us, and as we surrender to His breathtaking love for us, He will show us a love unimaginable! A love that is unconditional; a love that can only come from the One who created us.

Be SHOWERED BY HIS GRACE!

Epilogue

I walked by my favorite tree in the neighborhood recently and stopped in appreciation. I have admired this tree many times in passing, but on this occasion, it stood out in glorious splendor. The sun was shining on the gleaming white bark and I studied the tree, from the ground to the tips of the top branches, against the vivid blue sky.

The bottom of the tree was covered in gray bark and surrounded by unsightly brush. The lower branches showed some scattered patches of the white bark, and there were a few dead and broken limbs as well. As my eyes traveled up the trunk, more of the white bark was revealed and the branches were healthier. The top branches were almost solid white and displayed the fruit of the tree.

I felt God was speaking to my soul, as He revealed this tree as a picture of me. I started out as part of the world, surrounded by the ugliness of life, with no idea of what was inside. As I grew older and experienced different situations, I suffered from the effects of the world, brokenness and death, but something was happening on the inside and glimpses of the changes could be spotted here and there. As I have moved further along, greater refining has started taking place. I am now an older, more mature woman and fruit is beginning to come forth, as God reveals more of what has been hidden. The fruit will increase if I stay close to the Creator, who has also nourished this tree to its full height, which stands strong and majestic in the bright light of the sun. I, too, want to stand strong for the Lord; an empty vessel for the Son's light to shine through, to be useful in His service.

My daily prayer is to fulfill my destiny, while God continues His divine pruning. Excited anticipation grows with the changes, and I am filled with a renewed sense of purpose and direction. I believe and declare Ephesians 3:20 over my life that God will do immeasurably more than all I can ask or imagine! I cherish the good memories from the past, with gratitude for the steps that have brought me to my present. I am striving to finish strong in my journey, according to Philippians 3:13-14 NIV:

"Brothers and sisters, I do not consider myself yet to have taken hold of it. But one thing I do: Forgetting what is behind and straining toward what is ahead, I press on toward the goal to win the prize for which God has called me heavenward in Christ Jesus."

The journey continues.

◄ July 2007

July 2007 ►

◄ July 2007

◄ *Birthday*
October 2007

Scott 2008 ►

February 2008 ▶

◀ *Wedding*
October 2006

December 2008 ▶

About the Author

Iris Long shares "Showered By Grace" as her first published book. Before being called to write, she worked in medical transcription for thirty-five years. This mother, widow, and grandmother enjoys the mountains, serving at her local church, and ministering to others whom God brings across her path. Iris resides in Knoxville, TN.

Made in the USA
Columbia, SC
25 April 2021